Children of Men

Children of Men

Rose Zander

Pleasant Word (a division of WinePress Publishing, PO Box 428, Enumclaw, WA 98022) functions only as book publisher. As such, the ultimate design, content, editorial accuracy, and views expressed or implied in this work are those of the author.

ISBN 13: 978-1-4141-1108-7
ISBN 10: 1-4141-1108-8
Library of Congress Catalog Card Number: 2007906923

"How precious is your kindness, O God!
The CHILDREN OF MEN
take refuge in the shadow of your wings.

They have their fill of the prime gifts of your house;
from your delightful stream, you give them to drink.
For with you is the fountain of life."
Psalm 36 (35):8–10

Table of Contents

Prologue

Jalteva lies on a valley plateau, stretching into the foothills of pine-clad mountains of the Department of Francisco Morazán in Central Honduras. It has an area of five hundred acres of fertile land. A narrow, meandering river twists through and around these ample fields, finally spilling its waters into a deep lagoon.

Jalteva began as an agricultural center for poor and rebellious boys. With the forming of a juvenile law and the opening of a juvenile court in 1970, the center became known as Centro de Orientación Juvenil Jalteva. By then it was a haven and refuge for thousands of troubled boys—poor, neglected, rejected—victims of a society that considered them the unwanted scum of the earth.

Many of these boys were found wandering aimlessly on city and village streets. Vagabonding from place to place, they were always searching for something better in their lives. They were a hungry, scrawny lot, unkempt, disheveled, and parasite-ridden. Glue-sniffing helped them drift into their zombie world of oblivion to escape their misery. Petty thievery and their own acquired street wisdom brought survival in a tough world. Deserting classrooms created a vacuum of ignorance and nothingness—no values, no responsibilities, no idea of what life was really all about.

Gradually, these boys were ensnared by the seductive, inviting door which opened to them—the street gangs. Eager to belong and to be accepted, the boys submitted to the demands of a terrible initiation to prove that they were cool and merciless. They marked their bodies with gang symbols and tattoos. They found security, shelter, and companionship in living a life of delinquency. Yet they were trapped, bound by the rigid, unforgiving, and inescapable laws of gangland. They were young—boys between twelve and eighteen years of age—guided by older, long-term gang members. Fathered by these leaders, the boys suffered a different brutality, yet they belonged. The gang protected them. It was theirs.

Sinking deeper into the swamp of street life, the boys were dragged down and caught in the tangled web of mounting wrongdoing. For some, horrible crimes became commonplace. Some needed protection from brutal abuse on the streets or even in their own homes during their infrequent stays there. Some were orphaned. Some were violently snatched up by police, dumped into crowded holding cells, and stripped of the last shreds of their dignity. They were treated to beatings which raised welts and bruises and sometimes even drew blood. For questioning, their heads were shrouded in "capuchas," leather hoods that disoriented and almost suffocated the victims when pulled tight. Many boys "confessed" just to escape this torture.

Finally, the Junta Nacional de Bienestar Social (JNBS—the Junta), the welfare organization, began to rescue these boys from the adult prisons. The juvenile court heard their cases. Most of the boys were sent to Jalteva. This unique center could be theirs if they seized the opportunity to begin a new life. Here, there were no confining walls, high fences, or guard towers. There were no locked gates or armed guards. Solid brick buildings were spread over a nine-acre area. These were surrounded by playing fields and courts, fruit orchards, fishing lagoons, and fields for gardening and crops. This became an ideal home for the boys.

Life at the center touched on every aspect of a boy's needs—physical and psychological, moral and social, spiritual and cultural. Here, to start with, a boy recovered his health. Wholesome, simple but plentiful food fed his undernourished body. He learned to pray and to live with values. Discipline and respect became part of his life. He found love and dignity of person. He celebrated and enjoyed fun. All sports were his to choose from. He could run freely in the fresh country air and sunshine. Grade and high school classes educated him, as he picked up his studies where he had drifted off when he took to the streets. Shop training in one of the seven shops taught him a trade with skills for a future independent life. His special talents in art, theater, music, and crafts were developed. Individual and group counseling guided him through troublesome moments. Jalteva became a true haven for the boy.

For thirty-one years, I served as the educational orientator for these many boys. I mothered them, loved them, and attended their multiple needs, trying to make this new life a creative experience for them. Most responded in a magical way to each bit of attention. A few remained hostile and incorrigible, not wanting to yield to any gentle, tiny pushes in another direction.

The other personnel at the center were young men trained simply as primary school teachers. They eagerly took part in in-service courses in order to dedicate themselves more easily to the new challenges in their lives. I planned these courses. We read core books and met each week to discuss and apply the material found in these. The personnel, working directly with the boys as orientators and teachers, took correspondence courses from the national university to solidify their social, educational, and psychological skills in this difficult field of rehabilitation. They became the fathers the boys lacked in their lives. They were the men the boys could become. Today, this personnel continues the dedicated work of caring for the boys. As orientators and educators, they give new life, filled with future hope for the boys.

In this writing, I have chosen to tell the stories of twelve boys, selected from among the many which could be told. The incidents in the life of each boy are linked under a fictitious name to protect the individual. The pencil sketches try to capture the image of each boy created in the telling. The title for this collection was chosen from the Psalms, because these words summarize the spirit of Jalteva:

> How precious is your kindness, O God! The children of men take refuge in the shadow of your wings. They have their fill of the prime gifts of your house; from your delightful stream, you give them to drink. For with you is the fountain of life. (Ps. 36:8-10)

Return, O children of men. (Ps. 90)

Sister Rose Zander
School Sisters of St. Francis

Chapter One

Eduardo

Eduardo was a tall, strapping young lad of sixteen. The first time Sister Rose saw him, he was slumped against the doorframe of the social worker's office at Casamata, the main police headquarters of Tegucigalpa. His dark hair hung limp and long in a shaggy cut. His face was tearstained and angry. His breath came in jerky sniffles as he tried to control his tears. His red and white-striped T-shirt was soiled and pockmarked with tattered holes. Faded blue jeans hung low on his narrow hips. His wide, bare feet were dirty and calloused. He had just heard his mother, Maria del Carmen, deny him a place in her home. In a whining, shrill voice, she poured out her tale of woe to the social worker. She said Eduardo was "un bruto," a tough, rebellious kid. He was constantly at loggerheads with Antonio, her present "hombre," her live-in companion. If Eduardo didn't move out, Antonio would leave her. He was paying for the roof over their heads. If Antonio left, who would pay the rent? Who would support them and buy their food? Only Eduardo stood in the way.

The social worker offered various possible solutions and alternatives, but Maria del Carmen would hear none of it. She wanted Eduardo out of her life. Gone! To settle the case, a date was set for a court appearance in the juvenile court. The judge made the decision and assigned Eduardo to two years at Jalteva. At eighteen, he could return home or decide where he wished to live.

Deeply hurt emotionally and very angry with his mother, Eduardo arrived at Jalteva on a bright, sunny morning. He was filled with resentment. He isolated himself, refusing to talk to anyone. He skipped his classes and shop training. He only appeared for meals and at bedtime. He showed no interest in any of the activities, not even sports. He always stayed huddled by himself at the edge of his group.

One night, Eduardo slipped on the bathroom floor. As he fell, he hit his mouth on the edge of the sink, tearing his four front teeth loose from the gums. There was no nurse at the center nor any means of transportation to get Eduardo to a doctor. No buses circulated in the neighborhood at that hour. Personnel searched the area for a possible Good Samaritan willing to take the boy to Dr. Morel in Talanga. A passing truck was hailed, and the driver agreed to drop off the professor and Eduardo at the clinic, since he was going that way. Dr. Morel relieved the pain and pressured the teeth back into place. He recommended a liquid diet so the teeth could heal without disturbance. There was little else he could do. With painkillers and care, Eduardo healed well and didn't lose a single tooth.

Nearly a month later, Eduardo appeared for his regular session with Sister Rose. He sat in his usual sullen silence, head down, staring at his feet.

Suddenly, he lifted his head and burst out with, "I hate my mother!"

In a torrent of words, he spat out all his pent-up hatred and anger. His mother was a prostitute! She was only interested in men. He despised her and her men. The men passing through his life were his enemies. He fought with them. He rebelled against their dictates and had to fend for himself. The men only cared for his seven younger stepbrothers and stepsisters. Only they received attention. Besides, each one had a different father. He himself didn't even know who his father was, not even his name. Because he bad-mouthed his mother's men, he was frequently hit in the mouth or beaten bloody. Antonio had been the worst. Growing older, Eduardo said he tried to defend himself. Once, he was knocked down to the floor and cracked his head against the edge of a bench as he fell. He blacked out for a while. After a beating, he sometimes ran away for a few days. He begged on the streets or dug through garbage dumps. Sometimes he earned a few *centavos* carrying bundles for old ladies in the marketplace. Other times, he earned a few *lempiras* helping to load cargo trucks with sacks and boxes of produce from storehouses. When he returned home, it all started over again.

At this point in his flood of outpourings, Eduardo broke down in uncontrollable sobs. When he could again speak, he said that if his mother ever came to the center to visit him, he didn't want to see her. She should just stay away.

This spilling out of all his torments was the tiny beginning of healing for Eduardo. Sister Rose tried to help him understand that he could not continue hating or be unforgiving toward his mother. This would eat away and consume his inner spirit. And because his mother and his unknown father had given him life, he had to be grateful to them for his existence. Sister explained to him that he was now old enough to realize that he himself was able to choose what he wished to make of his life. What were his dreams? What did he want to become? Which path would he choose for himself? Sister suggested that he could begin by going to classes and selecting a shop to learn a trade. Eduardo agreed and said he was willing to try.

Eduardo had completed his first four primary school grades. Now he was registered in fifth grade. The librarian gave him his textbooks from the resource room. Eduardo collected his school supplies from the subdirector's office. That afternoon, Eduardo warily presented himself to the classroom.

The next morning, the shop supervisor took Eduardo on a tour of the shops. Each shop master explained the functioning of his shop. Eduardo chose carpentry as the trade he wanted to learn. He remained there for the rest of the morning.

On Friday, it was Eduardo's turn to sweep up the shop with two other companions. They wheeled their barrow-loads of shavings and wood scraps to the garbage dump. The trail followed the shallow irrigation ditch along the edge of the cornfield. The boys noted the fat, full ears of new corn. They made plans for a private corn roast the next day at the dump.

Watching for their opportunity after lunch on Saturday, Eduardo and his two friends swiped matches from the kitchen ledge. When all the other boys were well into their soccer match, the three adventurers crept away from the sidelines and disappeared into the tall grass along the trail to the garbage pit. They jumped the irrigation ditch and pilfered as many ears of corn as each could carry. Returning to the dump, they lit their fire in yesterday's wood shavings. Lying back, they enjoyed the tender, roasted ears of corn. They never noticed the fire slowly creeping toward the tall, dry grass. With a gust of wind and a fierce "whoosh," the grass caught and burst into flame. The fire raced madly to the west across the sun-scorched fields. The weeds, dried grass, and thorn brush quickly blossomed into high flames. It was still the dry season. For months there had been no rain. The fire had a free run.

Panic-stricken, Eduardo and his friends ran to the soccer field, screaming, "Fire! Fire!"

Everyone stopped playing in mid-game. All could see the billowing smoke in the distance. The ball was dropped. Some ran for buckets and washtubs for hauling water from the irrigation ditch. Groups ran for hoes, brooms, shovels, and rakes. Some simply tore low branches from trees as they ran toward the fire. These were used to beat out the edges of creeping flames. The firefighting went on almost all afternoon. Finally, three kilometers down the road, the fire was brought under control. The boys and personnel were all overheated and exhausted. Some had suffered blistered hands and minor burns from flying sparks. Clothing and faces were soot-streaked with grime and sweat.

A very angry neighbor met the boys and personnel, threatening them. His cattle corral was a smoldering circle of logs. The saving fact was that his cattle had been out grazing in another field, so they escaped becoming barbecued beef. At first, there was no reasoning with the man. He shouted and cursed the boys, blaming them for the fire. He demanded payment. Then, as he looked around, he calmed down. He realized that there were runaway fires all around him, climbing the mountainsides and raging through the pine forests. He dropped his claim and was grateful that at least his cattle had survived.

Eduardo and his culprit friends had a unique chore over the next few days. Under supervision, they had to rake burned remains into the center of the garbage pit. Then, they had to clear a meter-wide strip circling the heap. Next, they hauled in large stones, edging the rim of the circle with these to form "the ring." This would prevent future runaway fires. The gathered debris in the center heap was then set on fire. Using long, green branches as poles, the boys poked and moved the garbage remains until it was all ashes. As they worked, they looked longingly at the lush ears of corn in the field across the irrigation ditch. However, they didn't even dream of having another private corn roast.

Beehives set in long rows in the mango grove hummed with buzzing life. When the African bees swarmed northward, they homed in right on Jalteva's hives. A vicious mix formed and the bees churned in a sort of combat and simply went wild. Any person or animal crossing their paths felt their needle-hot stings. A field worker lost consciousness from the eight stings he received. One of the horses was covered in a rippling blanket of angry bees and was stung to death. The two German shepherds fled to the lagoon with a cover of bees clinging to their hair. The water saved them as they dove in. Once most of the African bees swarmed on, the remaining ones settled into Jalteva's hives. Because of the vicious strain, the hives had to be moved away from the center. They were settled deeply in the woods. Here they were unprotected. Vandals broke open the hives, stealing the honey. This sent the bees swarming in frantic, angry clouds, buzzing back to the main buildings. Some bees settled in huge clumps on branches of trees or bushes. Some hung from the warmth of the corridor lights like huge clusters of grapes. Others crawled through any crack or opening under the eaves, forming their honeycombs there.

Eduardo was fascinated by the bees. He loved to watch them swarm. He had great fun flinging stones at the clumps on the branches, enjoying the fast, desperate scattering of the bees before they collected into a swarming formation. He also loved honey. Whenever any of the workers tried to smoke out the bees after sunset, Eduardo was always there to help. If the attempt was successful, Eduardo reaped a large piece of honeycomb dripping with honey. But many times he paid a price by getting stung. He would then appear with an eye swollen shut, lips puffed up to a monstrous size, or an ear tripled in size and looking like a transparent balloon. Then Eduardo would hide under a towel like some desert sheik to cover his hideous appearance until the swelling disappeared and his face returned to normal. This didn't discourage him from enjoying the honey.

Eduardo was now eighteen. His two years at Jalteva were up. It was time for him to leave the center and return home. He didn't want to go. He had changed in many ways, although he had never forgiven his mother. Investigating the home for his return, the social worker found Antonio gone. Maria del Carmen was living with yet another man. Eduardo had another stepbrother. Eduardo did not want to live in that home.

Sister Rose helped Eduardo plan for his future. A small, reasonably priced room was found in a poor, but fairly safe barrio. Eduardo would live here with two other boys who also were leaving the center. They would share the rent. Scouting around with Eduardo, a day job was set up in a carpenter shop in Barrio Manchen. From his own savings account, Eduardo bought basic carpentry tools for his toolkit. A St. Vincent de Paul Conference in the States offered a scholarship for high school studies. Eduardo was registered for night classes in Instituto Nacional Cultural.

The day arrived. After classes closed in November, Eduardo said his farewell to the center. It was difficult for him to leave. He was frightened. Now he was on his own. The responsibilities were his alone. He had to begin the struggle to better his own life. He needed lots of support and encouragement to get over the rough spots. It wasn't easy. Many times, he almost despaired and wanted to give up. Sister Rose kept in touch. Each month, she visited him at his room, at his work, or at school. With each little push, he moved ahead and stuck tenaciously to his plan.

After five years, Eduardo had completed the course. He graduated as a public accountant. The lawyer's office where Eduardo had done his practice service hired him. He began to earn a good salary. When a better-paying job in a bank came along, the lawyer gave Eduardo a good recommendation. He could now move into a small apartment by himself.

One day, coming home on the bus, he stumbled into a young lady and knocked all her books to the ground. As he helped her pick them up, they bumped heads. After some laughter, they introduced each other. She was Zerina and was studying at the National University to become a social worker. She lived with her parents, just three blocks from Eduardo's apartment. They began seeing each other. The friendship soon blossomed into a closer relationship. They became engaged. After Zerina graduated as a social worker, the two set the date for a simple wedding.

Eduardo had won. His life was his own. He had fulfilled his dreams. A year and a half after the wedding, his wife presented him with a beautiful baby boy, Marco Tulio, a child who would know his father and be first in his mother's love.

Chapter Two

Lucas

Lucas lived in a small, one-room shack that clung precariously to the rugged mountainside in Barrio Reparto Arriba. It was a difficult climb over rocks and up a red-clay path to reach it. Lucas shared the home with his drunken mother, Amanda, and his five brothers and sisters. He was the oldest. He was a little tyke of ten, but was the size of a six-year-old. He was so small and undernourished. His huge, black eyes gazed soulfully out of his pale, thin face. His back and chest were marked with scars from cuts and cigarette burns, stark evidence of his mother's drunken rages. His hands, too, were covered with terrible burn scars. When he was eight years old, he had stolen forty *centavos* (about six cents) from his uncle. The uncle punished Lucas by tying his hands together. Then, he doused the hands with diesel and lit it. Lucas had to spend a month in the hospital and five more months at home, recovering. The terrible scars remained on his mutilated hands.

Notified of the abuse, the juvenile court removed Lucas from his home. He was placed in Jalteva for "protection." Physically, Lucas needed a great deal of attention. Recent bruises and cuts had become infected. He was taken to the lab at Rancho Santa Fe Clinic of Pequeños Hermanos. There he was tested. Among other things, five different types of encrusted parasites were found. One by one, these had to be treated, each with its specific medicine. Ridden of the parasites, Lucas received a month-long vitamin treatment. Now with nourishing food, simple but plentiful, Lucas began to fill out and grow.

Lucas was also in need of much loving attention. He had to overcome his fear of being severely punished for every little fault. He was a small, mischievous boy but didn't know how to be carefree about it. He always carried a look of dread on his face. It was months before he realized that no one was going to harm him physically or cause him pain, no matter what he did. He could begin to live and play as little boys should.

Lucas had completed his first and second grades, so he was placed in the third grade in the primary school. He did quite well, despite falling asleep frequently in class those first weeks. This was due to his exhausted, undernourished body.

For his shop, Lucas chose gardening. He loved working the soil and tucking seeds into the soft earth. He carefully watched over his planted vegetable seedbeds. He eagerly awaited the first sprouting of tiny green shoots. When the seedlings were big enough, he lovingly cradled each tiny plant in his hands. He transplanted it in its neat little hole, gently patting the soil around it to give it support. Finishing a row, Lucas stood, proudly admiring his evenly spaced plants set in a straight line like erect, miniature soldiers in orderly ranks. He weeded and watered. Each day, he searched the leaves for possible insect invaders. When any were found, they were attacked with a dusting of insecticide. At harvest time, Lucas gathered his produce and tied the vegetables into bundles to be delivered to the center's kitchen. Part of the payment for these went into Lucas' own savings account. The rest of the profit went into buying more seeds.

Lucas missed his mother and family, despite the harsh treatment he had always received on the part of his mother and uncle. One morning, just at daybreak, Lucas ran away. Somehow, he found his way back home over the long road—hiking, crossing fields, climbing mountain trails, and even hitching rides.

At home, Aunt Inez frequently kept watch over her sister Amanda's children. When Inez noticed that Lucas was home, she could appreciate how alive and well he looked, how he had grown, how happy he seemed. But then, after Lucas again experienced his mother's drunken rage, Aunt Inez easily convinced him to return to Jalteva. She herself traveled back with Lucas.

In Jalteva, the boys were divided into dormitory homes according to their ages. Each dormitory has distinct, colored panels beside each door. Lucas was assigned to Dormitorio Morado (the Purple Dorm). He lived there with thirty smaller boys, the ten-to-twelve-year-olds. One day, the feisty youngsters created a disastrous uproar in their dorm. Jaime took a machete and split open Lucas' bedside clothes cupboard. Marcos grabbed a hoe from the corner and smashed the padlock on the storage closet door. Not to be outdone, Wilfredo sliced open someone's suitcase. Others joined in, scattering clothing around on the floor. Some began tearing seams apart. Shoes became the next target. Shoestrings were ripped from the eyelets and swiped. Two hot-tempered boys lashed out at each other, scuffling for possession of a blue sports shirt.

The uproar caught the two professors in charge of the dorm unawares. What had begun as a sudden outburst quickly flamed into an all-out, uncontrolled near-riot. With a loud blast on a whistle, everyone stopped dead in their tracks. A curt order from one of the professors rang out and all the boys marched off into the living room, leaving behind the shambles. It took a long session to sort everything out and to restore order. Questioning revealed that Jaime had started it all. He admitted that he was angry at Lucas because Lucas hadn't shared the candy he had won as a prize. That was why Jaime had split Lucas' cupboard door. He was going to grab a fistful of candy. He didn't realize copycats would join in, delighting in the splintering and crashing noises. Assignments were given. The boys from the carpenter shop had to work with their master to repair the split clothes cupboard and the closet door. The sewing shop fellows had to sew up torn seams and mend ripped clothing. The shoemakers had to repair the slice in the suitcase. Then, the final punishment. No one could watch television for a week.

At daybreak, Lucas ran off again to his mother. Once more, Aunt Inez brought him back to the center the next day.

Creative scams were never lacking. A bartering racket, interchanging things for favors done, was organized by Lucas and his companions. You do this for me and I'll give you two tortillas. Or, I'll do your cafeteria cleaning for two days if you give me your new T-shirt.

One day at breakfast, Lucas was really hungry and wouldn't fork over the cheese he had promised Jorge for taking out the bathroom garbage. Very angry, Jorge threw his chair across the table at Lucas. In one wide swipe, the chair carried the plate of food and the coffee of an innocent neighbor right off the table as the boy jumped aside. So a third angry boy entered the food-slinging contest. Then Sister Rose stepped in. She ordered Lucas and Jorge to clean up the mess. Jorge refused. Sister grabbed him by the arm and practically dragged him to the mop. Taking it, Jorge slashed the mop back and forth over the mess and then threw the mop. He returned to the table and picked up his plate of food and his coffee. He threw them at Lucas, who was still mopping. Lucas ducked. The food and coffee splattered onto the back of an older boy at the next table. Another angry, but bigger boy rose to the defense. Sister Rose grabbed Jorge and gave him five good swats on his behind. He was so shocked that all fight went out of him. Alone, he did the final, good cleanup of the mess he had created. Then he sadly looked at the remains of his breakfast—one lonely tortilla sitting in a puddle of cold coffee. Being hungry, Jorge ate it anyway.

Lucas always enjoyed swimming and fishing. He was extremely happy every time his group went on an outing to Rio Grande. This long, clear, swift-flowing river is delightful for swimming and just splashing about. Some pools that formed on the rounded curves were great for fishing. On this outing, tired of swimming, Lucas and a few friends hiked downriver. They discovered a snug little orchard filled with luscious papaya and mango trees, plus a patch of golden, ripe pineapples. It belonged to a solitary, little old lady whose face was a mass of deep wrinkles. Her shack was on the upper edge of the orchard. With Lucas in the lead, the boys raided the orchard, stuffing themselves with the goodies they had found. Then they filled their pockets with mangos and their arms with papaya and pineapples. The sharp eyes of the lady discovered them. She began to shout and scold. The boys hooted back and started to run with their loot. The lady was defenseless, but the echo of her scolding followed the boys along the river's edge.

The boys were met by their professor, who had been out searching for them. It was time to return to the center. What an unpleasant surprise when he saw all the fruit! Questioning the boys, he quickly calculated the cost of the stolen fruit. There was no time to return to the old lady and settle accounts, but each boy had to dole out three *lempiras* ($1.50) from his shop savings account. On the next group's outing the following day, a delegation of boys delivered the raiders' money to the little old lady. She was hugely surprised, having never expected payment. Very satisfied and grateful, she gave the boys a ripe pineapple to share.

Lucas' regular running away to his home continued. His Aunt Inez just as regularly brought him back to the center. Lucas had reached sixth grade, almost completing his primary school education. One day he disappeared again. This time, after visiting his drunken mother, he evaded his Aunt Inez. He never returned to Jalteva. He wasn't heard from again—one more boy lost to the great nowhere.

Chapter Three

Fernando

Poverty brought Fernando to Jalteva as a twelve-year-old. He was a sturdy child, despite the unstable conditions of his home. His mother, Luisa, was a tired, worn woman. Her life had been one long, hard struggle. Since the age of eleven, she had spent her days on the streets, vending a variety of breads from a large, woven basket balanced on her head. Her eldest son, Tonio, was in and out of the central penitentiary. He was physically ill with intestinal problems due to parasites and the bad diet in prison. His troubles with the law continued to multiply. His teenage wife and his son added to the burden of his own mother. Luisa cared for them along with Fernando and a younger daughter. She alone held this responsibility. The father of her three children had deserted her long ago.

All shared a one-room hovel which clung leaning into the rugged mountainside in Las Colinas, above Barrio Manchen. Cracks in the floorboards opened to the humid soil beneath the home. Wind and dust sifted through the ill-fitting wall planks, peppering everything with a gray powder. Rain seeped in, forming dirty puddles where wall and floor met. The only furniture was a narrow bed frame. Over its bare springs, cardboard boxes had been flattened as a covering instead of a mattress. Luisa and the girls slept here. The boys slept curled up on the floor, huddling together for warmth. There were no blankets or other bedding. A small adobe stove was cramped into the far corner. One lone, battered kettle sat there for heating water or for any cooking. A loop of coarse twine was strung from nail to nail in the corner above the bed. The few clothes anyone possessed were draped haphazardly over this.

Fernando tried to help out by carrying bundles and doing odd jobs in the marketplace, bringing in a few extra *lempiras*. However, what he really wanted to do was study. His mother made various visits to the Junta, the welfare organization responsible for child and family care. Luisa often sold sweet breads to the office workers. She never lost an opportunity to mention Fernando and his great dream of going to school some day. On this special day, one social worker bought her usual sweet bread for her morning coffee break. She became interested in Fernando. She questioned Luisa about her son. Answers were eagerly given. Fernando was a good boy, healthy, very intelligent, a hard worker, responsible. Luisa was just too poor to send him to school.

The social worker set a date for visiting the home. She met Fernando and had to agree he was deserving of a chance for a better life. At headquarters, she began to gather all necessary papers and documents, filled in the forms and a formal petition for the court. She presented these to the juvenile judge, who approved the case. Fernando could go to Jalteva until his eighteenth birthday.

At Jalteva, Fernando adapted well. Because he was so serious and looked older than his years, his companions nicknamed him "Abuelo" (Grandfather), which stuck to him all during his stay at the center. He set quite a record for himself. He learned two trades in shops—sewing and barbering. He completed his primary school education and maintained an excellent grade average. He was remarkable in sports, earning a spot on all the center's official teams in soccer, basketball, and volleyball. He was most proud of his role as a monitor for a group of the younger boys.

Many a time, this group of boys led Fernando on a tiring chase down to an old swimming hole below the retaining wall of the large lagoon. There, hidden away along the river rocks, the little fellows hunted for crabs and stuffed them into their pockets. No one ever had to ask where they had been. Their bare, muddy feet and the wet areas around their pants' pockets were dead giveaways. Sometimes, too, wiggling claws scrabbled over the edges of a pocket, and a crab tumbled to the floor during a class. The clicking gait of the escapee caught everyone's attention, including that of the teacher. A disturbance was created when the boys would dive for the creature. By the end of class, the professor might have four or five crabs scrabbling around in a box on his desk. After class, one of the culprits had to take the box and deposit the crabs back along the river. The boys whose crabs had escaped were very disappointed because this meant they couldn't take part in the planned evening ritual. This was lighting a fire behind the dormitory. Then the crabs were boiled in an old vegetable oil can. The boys shared drinking the broth and having a bedtime snack, sucking the crab meat from the claws.

One morning, five of Fernando's little fellows were missing from shop. He found them hunting crabs by the river. Pockets were checked and crabs were dumped. The five culprits, under Fernando's supervision, spent the afternoon dragging the large, recently cut African palm branches from the plaza to the garbage ring on a rocky ledge along the river's edge.

Fernando also taught some of his boys how to be shepherds. They took turns in pairs shepherding the flock to keep the sheep within their pasture area. They had to be kept away from the laurels and other ornamental plants along the sidewalks and around the buildings. The sheep loved to nibble on these and in no time could strip every bush bare if left to do so.

Problems arose on some days. Stray dogs went after the sheep. On one sad day, a ewe and her lamb were killed. Another ewe tried to save her twin lambs. One lamb was killed and the ewe was badly mauled. She died a few days later. The twin survivor had to be bottle-fed by the boys. Whenever it was hungry, the lamb faithfully came to the kitchen door and bleat until someone appeared with its bottle. When the door was open, the lamb walked right in and bleated until fed.

Fernando had a difficult time keeping the Christmas tree lights lit on the trees in the boys' dormitory and in the main hall. Two of the little fellows had a craze for unscrewing four or five of the tiny colored lights from their small sockets on a string of lights. They carried these around in their pockets. It made them feel like they were in possession of something. Every little while, they took the lights from their pockets and enjoyed the array of colors. It was a continuous fight with these boys to screw the lights back in place and leave them there so that the string of lights would function. With that task accomplished, Fernando had the boys stand back and admire the beauty of an entire tree lit in color, seeing in this way the difference between the dead bulbs in the hand and lit ones on the tree.

The next big battle was over slingshots. The little boys began cutting the tongues out of other boys' shoes. In the carpenter shop, on the sly, they made their forked pieces of wood from scraps lying around. Next, they negotiated trades with neighbors passing along the road to get their packet of rubber bands for attaching the leather tongue. Soon the boys were slinging stones in all directions. Birds were killed, especially doves, which were excellent for roasting over open fires. Roofing got cracked and windows were broken. Sometimes an unsuspecting head got split when a stone found the wrong target. This had to stop. Fernando, with help from personnel and other older boys, began confiscating slingshots. Later, any boy still found with a slingshot and stones in his pocket had to pick up fifty stones of slingshot size and deposit them down by the river. All slingshots were stored with the camping equipment for hunting only on camping trips.

Working in the fields one day, while preparing the soil for a garden plot, Fernando and his older companions got quite a scare. When the pick Fernando was using brought up a huge hunk of dirt, it uncovered bones! Exploring further, Fernando gave a yell when he saw what looked like a skull. It was a human skeleton! All work halted. The boys and personnel crowded around and simply stared. The director was informed. He sent a driver to Cedros for the forensic doctor. Meanwhile, the boys all sat waiting in the shade along the field's edge.

Studying the bones and the scraps of clothing, the doctor thought the remains belonged to a man of about forty to fifty years of age. There was a bullet hole in the back of the skull. The doctor calculated that the remains had been there for some years. The Talanga police were called. They searched the entire field area, fearing this discovery might be one of the many clandestine burial places of persons who had disappeared over the years in Honduras. For days, the field was off limits and guarded. Units of police dug up almost the entire field, but no more bones were found. The skeleton appeared to be that of a solitary murder victim, who was never identified.

One holiday, Fernando was on stage in the main hall helping set up things for a dramatization. Waiting boys were leaning against the grand piano. In passing, Fernando touched a key. As the musical note sounded, the entire piano collapsed with a booming crash onto the floor. Stunned, everyone stood stock still. Fernando kept repeating that he had only touched one key. The music teacher examined the wreckage. To his surprise, he discovered that the three supposedly sturdy, pegged piano legs had been eaten clean through by termites.

Other endless adventures, hard work, and study filled Fernando's years at Jalteva. He was now eighteen years old. It was time for him to leave the center and take up a life on his own. Plans were made and he returned home. Scouting around Comayaguela with Sister Rose, he found work at a sewing shop, La Fama, on Calle Real. Fernando received a scholarship from a group of U.S. students. Sister got him registered in night school at Instituto Nacional Cultural.

Work went well. Fernando used his earnings wisely. He bought a mattress for the old bed frame and a rollaway cot for the boys. Woolly blankets were gotten so each could keep warm at night. A small pinewood table and four simple stools were added to the furnishings. Before acquiring the stools, Fernando would run to a neighboring shack and borrow a chair whenever Sister Rose visited. On one visit, she noticed a frying pan and a teakettle accompanying the lonely, battered kettle on the adobe stove.

As things improved the following year, Fernando moved his family higher up the mountain to a larger shack which sat on a level spot. It was one, long room, but snug. No more dust, wind, or rain blew in. Fernando sewed muslin curtains as room dividers. He hung these across the room on thick twine cords, separating the sleeping quarters from the living area.

After five years, Fernando completed his high school education as a certified public accountant. He found an excellent job in the bank where he had done his social service practice. He moved up in rank to better-paying positions. Finally, he became an auditor in the top government ministry, helping to control the administration of government offices.

At age thirty, Fernando met and married the woman with whom he wanted to share his life. She worked selling tickets at one of Tegucigalpa's large movie theaters. One son has blessed their marriage. Fernando moved his family a third time into a humble brick home in a central barrio near San Felipe Hospital. Life has become easier for Fernando, and his mother no longer has to sell bread on the streets.

Chapter Four

Marcos

Night had already fallen when the truck returned from Tegucigalpa. After a short stop, the new boy was left standing with the night guard at the gatehouse of Jalteva. In a swirl of dust, the truck rumbled off to the kitchen to unload the week's food supply.

The boy, disoriented, stood clutching tightly his battered plastic bag, lumpy with his few earthly possessions. When he was asked his name, it took a few minutes before he could recall and stutter out his name, Marcos. He was a tall, handsome lad of fourteen. His fine-featured face was very pale, dominated by huge, dark eyes, which constantly viewed the world with a look of total confusion. He was physically and mentally damaged. His capacity to respond readily was dulled by years of glue sniffing and the inhaling of other volatile substances.

Awakening the next morning, after a restless night and with an unquenchable need for something to sniff, Marcos couldn't quite remember where he was. How did he get here? In the rush of rising and dressing among the many strange boys around him, he began to remember. Something about the marketplace and a policeman. He had swiped a small can of glue from a shoemaker's bench in the marketplace. Running from the angry shouts of the man, Marcos stumbled and collided with a policeman. Marcos was caught by the collar of his shirt and relieved of his little treasure. This was returned to a winded, indignant shoemaker, who had managed to puff his way to the spot. Marcos was hauled off roughly to Casamata and closed in a holding cell with other street boys. Now he was here in Jalteva.

The day began for Marcos with many interviews. Classes and shop choices were explained to him. He had difficulty coordinating his thoughts. He didn't know what to choose. He felt lost. As soon as he could, he escaped from the boy showing him around the center. He isolated himself, which he did frequently. He began searching for something to inhale. He disappeared. Searching boys finally found him spaced out like a zombie in a corner of the pig stable. He was sucking on oranges he had swiped from the citrus grove. He said he was thirsty. Next to him was a tin can with diesel fuel in it. He had siphoned this from the tractor's fuel tank so he could inhale the fumes.

On another day, Marcos was found in a back field by a field worker. He was doubled over in pain. He had mounted bareback on one of the cattlemen's horses. When he had dismounted, the horse had bucked and kicked him in the groin. Recovering from the pain, Marcos picked up a large rock and chased after the horse, swearing he was going to kill the animal. Not succeeding and frustrated, Marcos disappeared again in a fit of fury. He usually reappeared at mealtime or bedtime, but this night he didn't.

In the pitch black of night and armed with flashlights, groups of older boys and personnel turned out to search for him. At last, he was found sprawled along the edge of the swimming lagoon by the citrus grove. With much coaxing, he was brought back to the dormitory and shoved into a cold shower. The water cleared away the mud and some of the haze left by his diesel sniffing and fury. The orientator got him into bed. On her rounds, the nurse sedated him to keep him settled for the night.

In the morning, Marcos went to the carpenter shop, the shop he had finally chosen for learning a trade. As always at lunchtime, the shop master checked the pockets of his boys to make sure no one was leaving with glue, large nails sharpened to knifelike points, broken bits of coping saws, or any other tools. Marcos wouldn't let the master search his pockets. This was reported to the orientator, who then did the search in the general formation line. A plastic bag with glue was found tucked in the waistband of his undershorts. It was enough glue to send him off into space again. The glue was confiscated. In exchange, Marcos got the task of cleaning the cafeteria after each meal for a week.

It continued to be a difficult time for Marcos, trying to adapt to a disciplined program, plus the daily schedule without his glue crutch. His wandering, isolating himself, and searching for glue or other substances continued. Despite all the vigilance, he was often found with a plastic bag of glue tucked away in his shirt front, handy for continual, hidden sniffs.

On certain holidays, a wiener roast was held at the evening meal as a special treat to celebrate. Bonfires were lit in the dormitory avenue. Each boy found a slender green branch shaved to a point to use as his roasting fork. Some daredevils among the boys thought it might be an interesting challenge to see who could jump over a bonfire. Observing this and without further thought, Marcos tried to imitate this stunt. In his uncoordinated way, he took off, leaped into the air, slipped, and fell into the blaze. Boys and professors pulled him out and frantically beat out the smoldering patches. They dragged him off quickly to the shower and doused him until he was soaked all over. Then they stripped off his clothes, letting the cold water wash over the scorched spots on his body. Surprisingly, his burns weren't too bad. The worst burn was on his right thigh. Lesser burns covered his right knee and ankle. Later, the nurse plastered these with Unguentine-soaked sterile gauzes.

Desperate for something to inhale, Marcos experimented one day with OKO, an insecticide that each dormitory used to control insect invaders. Marcos got no results inhaling it, so he drank some. He was one sick boy. In panic he ran off into the night. Again, a search group went after him. He was found up in the branches of the huge mango tree. He was forced to drink a warm milk treatment to soothe his burned throat and to get him to vomit. All through the night, a watch was kept over him as he suffered through the crisis.

Gradually, Marcos began to stick with his group. He began to take an interest in some activities. He still needed individual tutoring in an effort to restore some of the damage caused by his addiction. Continual memory exercises were part of his program. With less and less glue to feed his addiction, Marcos began to notice more of his surroundings and to make friends with some of the other boys.

One day Marcos and his friends found a nice fat armadillo in a weed patch. After pouncing on it, they took it to the kitchen after killing it. The cooks prepared the delicious delicacy in a soup with the sweet-tasting meat served on tortillas. The hard, scaly shell was kept as a souvenir on the dividing ledge in their dormitory.

Padre Ivan Betancourt often used Jalteva as a rest stop on his trips to and from Juticalpa. He enjoyed spending time with the boys, sometimes celebrating Mass. On one stop six months before he was assassinated by rich landowners and the military, Ivan left his huge German shepherd, Skippy, with the boys. Marcos became very attached to the dog and gave it special care. On a picnic outing to Guaimaca, Marcos begged to take Skippy along. The other boys eagerly helped lift the dog onto the back of the truck. The long ride was too much for the poor creature. Skippy got sick. Arriving in Guaimaca, Skippy fled into the woods.

When it was time to return to the center, nobody could find Skippy. The dog answered no calls, not even those of Marcos. The boy was heartbroken when the truck left without Skippy. Apparently, the dog didn't care for another rough ride on the back of the truck with the boys. Weeks later, some forest people notified the center that they had found the dog. Two of the professors went in the pickup truck to bring Skippy home. This time the dog got to ride in the cabin. What joy for both dog and boys, especially for Marcos! Skippy was wolfishly hungry and gobbled down whatever the boys offered. Marcos even shared his Posada cookies with Skippy.

Then there was a mishap in the carpenter shop. Marcos caught his left hand in the circular saw. The tip of his middle finger was badly mangled and the ring finger was deeply sliced. No nurse at the center! Sister Rose got the bleeding under control and the old truck lumbered off to the emergency room of Escuela Hospital in Tegucigalpa. The doctor had to amputate part of the middle finger but was able to save the other completely. It took lots of special care, but both fingers healed well.

One evening, Marcos had a relapse. He had found a bottle of paint thinner, which he greedily and secretly inhaled. When the dorm orientator discovered him, the bottle was taken away. Marcos went wild. He went after the professor, who had locked the dormitory door when he left to dispose of the thinner. He didn't want Marcos running off again. The boy kicked the door fiercely, screaming insults and obscenities.

Hearing this, Sister Rose went to see what was going on. She couldn't get in because the door was locked. She tracked down the professor and together they entered the dormitory. Five boys were trying to wrestle Marcos to the floor, but he fought them off, punching, kicking, and screaming. Sister Rose ordered the boys to stand back. They wouldn't let go, saying that Marcos had a knife. Finally, though, the boys stepped back. Sister grabbed Marcos by the arm and tugged him outside. She got him walking up and down the central plaza at a fast pace to work off his hysteria and anger. Then she sat him down on the office steps, talking softly to him, coaxing him to give up the knife. After a while, he pulled the knife from his sock and handed it to Sister.

Returning to the dormitory, Marcos raced off ahead of Sister. He stopped at the door of the professor's room, and again began to kick and scream insults and foul threats. This time, the boys dragged Marcos outside and right into the path of the director. He, with Sister Rose, sat trying to calm Marcos, soft-talking him out of his fury. Soon, Marcos was calm enough to return to his dormitory. The dorm orientator got Marcos into the shower and then into bed. Marcos zonked out immediately, exhausted from his most recent rampage.

After sleeping off most of the effects of the thinner, Marcos was a bit groggy the next day. He didn't do well in class. He couldn't concentrate nor remember what was being taught. Most of his morning was spent in orientations with Sister Rose and counseling with the psychologist. Marcos didn't quite grasp the happenings of the night before. By afternoon, he was almost back on even keel. He went to his carpenter shop, but the master made sure he didn't touch any machinery.

The technical council met to evaluate Marcos' case. The group decided to eliminate classes and just assign Marcos full time to shop. With repeated practice, he might be able to make simple furniture and so earn his livelihood on leaving the center. Strict vigilance would have to be kept to prevent him from swiping glue and other substances used in the shop.

After a successful year in just shop, Marcos was again assigned to the classroom. Somehow, he had reached sixth grade before entering Jalteva, despite his glue-sniffing sprees. Now he wanted to see if he could complete his primary school education. He struggled. He was tutored by a Lansing,

Michigan, university student during her six months at the center as a volunteer. Marcos did better but didn't make the grade.

During the next year, his second in sixth grade, he did manage to just squeak through, graduating at last from the primary school.

In one way, Marcos was very lucky. He had both a mother and a father who were very concerned about him. They came once or twice a month to visit him, always bringing his younger sisters and brothers along. Happy with the improvement in Marcos, his parents hoped that he could soon come home. He was now going on seventeen. The father had his own carpenter shop and was hoping Marcos could work with him there when he did come home. Marcos wasn't planning to go to high school. He did like working with wood, though, and was doing fine producing simple furniture.

Evaluations were written up from each department and given to the technical council for the final decision. It was favorable. Marcos, having the support of his family, was going home. The juvenile court gave the final approval and the document releasing Marcos from Jalteva, and he went home.

Doing follow-up, Sister Rose visited his home in Barrio Morazán. It was a humble plank structure wedged between two shops on the main street climbing the hill through the barrio. It was one long room, about eight yards long and two yards wide. The floor was of hard-packed dirt. Marcos proudly greeted Sister and then surprised her by showing off his first completed production in carpentry. It was a triple-decker bunk bed, tightly fitted in the space just behind the entrance door. Marcos explained that his three sisters slept in the lower bunk.

One of Marcos' brothers interrupted, proudly announcing, "We live on the second floor," meaning his brother and he slept on the middle bunk.

Marcos slept on the third tier of the bunk bed. The parents slept on a cot aligned against the wall at the foot of the children's bunk bed. A long, narrow table was pushed against the opposite wall, leaving about a foot of walking space in between. Under the table were six small, low stools. At mealtime, two always perched on the edge of the cot while eating.

Just inside the back door was the usual *lorena*, the adobe stove accommodating a frying pan and a kettle. Outside was a small patio, sheltering a cement laundry sink that was handy for washing dishes. Tucked neatly at one end was the family's carpenter shop, where Marcos worked with his father. Always fascinated by the handling of wood, Marcos held on to what he had gained at Jalteva: control over his glue-sniffing addiction. Even though he was still marked with a studied slowness in his responses and actions, Marcos was basically healthy and happy. He was fitting in and doing well with his family. He would find his place in society.

Chapter Five

Chico

The boy was found wandering the dusty country roads of southern Honduras. He was disheveled, long-haired, filthy, and wearing frayed clothing. His wide feet were bare and calloused. He was short and stocky, bewildered by all around him, yet a constant, innocent grin curved his mouth.

For days now, Margarita, a Baptist missionary, had been observing him. Her curiosity finally won out. One day, she met the boy head-on, blocking his meandering path. She greeted him. His response was a grunt and a half-laugh. She asked him his name. Another half-laugh was his only response. The boy was mute.

After trying many approaches, Margarita gave up on the questioning. She took the boy by the arm and gently coaxed him along with her. Grinning and docile, he shuffled along with her to the Baptist mission center. There she consulted with the team, and the group became interested in Margarita's find. Having gotten no name nor a single word from the boy, Margarita suggested that meanwhile they call him "Chico," a short form of Francisco.

Chico was introduced to water and soap in the shower. Next, from the wardrobe, Margarita sorted out some clothing for him. No shoes were found for his oversized feet. All these new experiences were accompanied with grunts and laughter. When Chico was all spruced up, he was seated at the dining room table and served a variety of food. A bigger grin covered Chico's face as he dug in with his fingers, ignoring the fork and spoon. He gulped the milk. With a grunt, he motioned for more.

At the Baptist center's clinic, a visit to the doctor proved that Chico was healthy. No cause was found for his not talking. The doctor calculated that according to his bone structure, Chico must be between fourteen and sixteen years of age.

No one could discover from him where he had originated. During the next few days, Margarita took Chico with her, walking through the streets of the nearby town, asking questions, hoping someone could identify or claim Chico. No one did.

Next, Margarita placed a description and a photo of Chico in the daily paper. Again, no one responded. On her next trip to Tegucigalpa, Margarita took Chico and all the results of her investigation plus the doctor's reports to the Junta, the welfare organization responsible for children and families. Chico was deposited at their observation center.

This was a first for this center. No one could decide what to do with Chico—mute, grinning, making loud belly laughs, and running in circles! The boy remained a mystery to them. There was no place prepared to care for children with Chico's problems. Then someone was "inspired" and came up with the brilliant suggestion that Chico be sent to Jalteva, the center for troubled, delinquent boys. So Chico arrived at Jalteva. No one there had been prepared either for handling a case like his.

One of Chico's first behaviors witnessed at Jalteva was his gleeful circling at a fast run wherever a group was assembled—for morning prayer, a conference, or even Mass. He burst into the hall, circled it at a run, whooping away in loud belly laughs, startling everyone by this unexpected interruption. Personnel and boys jumped to their feet and tried to snag Chico as he zoomed by. Nabbing him, they steered him toward the door. Outside, he had wide open spaces in which to run and laugh. Speakers, visitors, or the priest had to be warned that this might happen, and not to get upset nor excited, to just keep moving along, ignoring the distraction. If Chico had been coaxed to sit on a bench at the back, no one knew when he might begin his loud laughter and running. Keeping him quiet wasn't easy.

The rains began. Everything was soggy and muddy. All the boys had wet feet inside their wet shoes (if they had shoes). Chico always found the biggest puddle to splash through and the muddiest patch to trek across. He got such pleasure hearing the splash and squish his feet made or the feel of the muddy ooze between his toes.

Another of his rather expensive pleasures he simply could not resist was the shattering crash of glass breaking. He threw stones at windowpanes until one broke. Then he laughed uproariously as the glass splintered to the ground. In all, Chico cost the center more than seventy windowpanes during his stay.

Chico was fascinated by the loose flapping of cloth. He pulled the sewing out of the seams of his pants and shirts. Then he marched along, enjoying the flap of the hanging panels of cloth against his body.

Sister Rose spent time working alone with Chico each day to see what might be drawn from his speechless world. She gave him drawing paper and brightly colored markers. Chico meticulously drew an amoebic shape. He carefully filled in the sprawling form with a brilliant color. Then he topped the color over with solid black, hiding the lovely color completely. Never once did he color outside the line of his shape, always leaving a perfectly neat, black amoeba. Sister saved these drawings to show to psychologists. She wanted to know if these professionals could give an explanation or meaning to Chico's artwork. No one ever gave a satisfactory answer. Sister concluded that maybe this was Chico's way of showing that colors existed in his world but that he was hiding them behind a black screen.

One day, Sister Rose tried another exercise. She gave Chico a pair of scissors and some simple geometric figures on a paper. She wanted to see if he could follow cutting lines as carefully as his drawing lines. Chico wasn't interested. Instead, he grabbed the scissors and began cutting tufts of hair from his head. Before Sister could get the scissors away from him, his head looked like that of a chewed rabbit.

Next, Sister Rose began to show Chico one-word pictures, trying to get him to pronounce the words after her. At last, the first words were spoken, after much effort. Only a few were remembered and with a different recognition. Any figure or person in a skirt was "mama." Any figure or person in pants, whether man or woman, was "papa." Any animal with four legs was "a horse," whether the picture showed a cow, pig, or dog. Chico now had a speaking vocabulary of three words.

Soon Chico recognized and called Sister Rose "Sister." He began calling his mentally handicapped friend by name, "Orlando." Next Chico picked up a few verbs but always spoke in third person. He used his name with the verb, never "I"—"Chico take," "Chico come," never speaking in full sentences. It was a small victory.

At the Palm Sunday celebration, each boy brought his palm branch and flowers to the procession. Someone got these for Chico. He spent the entire liturgy being quiet, but he enjoyed the continual swishing and waving of his palm branch during the ceremony. Sounds had become a great pleasure for him.

On Holy Saturday morning, it had become the tradition at the center for the smaller boys to color the Easter eggs for their nests. Chico was invited to help. Again, color attracted him. He watched the others for a while. One boy then helped Chico juggle the first egg into his red dye. Then Chico wanted to put an egg in everyone else's color. Finally, he understood that "red" was his color and stayed by his cup, dipping out colored eggs and replacing each with another white one. He seemed almost surprised to see a red egg in place of the white one he had just placed in the dye.

In the evening of Holy Saturday, at the Vigil of Light, Chico grabbed four candles from the box. When he was caught with four instead of one, he pitched all four candles into the laurel bushes. Another boy quickly retrieved them and gave only one back to Chico. Could Chico be trusted with a lighted candle? Sister Rose assigned another boy to keep a close watch on Chico. Again, he was quiet throughout the long ceremony, eyes glued to the flame of his lighted candle. He didn't like it when the candles were blown out.

He kept repeating, "Chico light. Chico light."

As the first year of coping with Chico moved into the second year, the Junta still had done nothing to resolve Chico's problems. No appropriate place had been found for him. He was changing. He was getting chubby. He hardly ever ran in circles anymore. He was becoming a young man, mustache and all. He began to curl up in any corner of any room and go to sleep on the floor. The library, behind the book stacks, was one of his favorite places, especially when lots of boys were using the library. He seemed to want people nearby. It seemed to make him feel secure.

Often, he would sneak into the director's office during sessions of the technical council. Taking two chair cushions, he placed them behind the door and lay down. After falling asleep, he was soon snoring away. The council members just smiled and continued with their session. Before leaving and locking up any room, a check had to be made to make sure that Chico wasn't asleep in some hidden corner.

A decision was made. The psychologist of the center met with the director of Ciudad Blanca, a center for homeless men. They lived in groups, doing gardening, raising bees, making craft items, and doing other manual activities for self-support. A plan was worked out to transfer Chico to Ciudad Blanca on a trial basis. One of the main reasons was that Chico was becoming very aggressive with smaller boys, who loved to bother and tease him. One day, angered by teasing, Chico grabbed a smaller boy and knocked his head against a brick wall. The boy's forehead split open. A visiting nurse, the wife of one of the professors, stitched up the cut. The next day, the transfer plan was finalized, and on Saturday the psychologist traveled to Ciudad Blanca with Chico. He helped Chico settle in and then left for Jalteva.

After Sunday liturgy the next day, the unbelievable happened. The boys were all at breakfast when in burst Chico. Somehow, he had found his way back to Jalteva. How had he gotten on the right bus? How had he known that he had to hike up the two kilometers to the center from the bus stop? Possibly someone at Ciudad Blanca had put him on the bus when the men at that center didn't know what to do with this young man, Chico, who wasn't talking or reacting in a normal fashion. Whatever had happened, one thing was certain. The trial transfer had failed.

The next move was an effort to get authorization from headquarters to have Chico admitted to Santa Rosita, the country's mental institution. This really wasn't the right place for Chico because of the attention he needed, but it was the best that could be done for the time being.

After being admitted, tests were done and Chico remained at Santa Rosita. Personnel from Jalteva and a social worker from the Junta visited Chico regularly. He was unhappy and listless. He didn't want to stay there. He was getting thin. His case was unique. There was no special place found to give him the individual and specialized care he needed.

Sad as it may seem, when personnel visited Chico again at Santa Rosita, he was not there. The institution had "released" him, saying that Santa Rosita could do nothing for him. Where he had gone, no one knew. Where to begin searching for him, no one knew. In all probability, Chico is again wandering the dusty roads of southern Honduras.

Chapter Six

Mateo

The call came from the juvenile court in Comayagua. There were eleven fifteen-to-eighteen-year-old gang members ready to enter Jalteva. Ten boys were in the holding cell at the Comayagua jail. The eleventh boy, Mateo, was to be picked up at St. Theresa's Hospital. The ten had savagely attacked him the week before because he had betrayed them. The police had raided the old warehouse the boys were using as storage for their easy, money-making thefts. All their TVs and CD and VCR players, sound equipment, jewelry, and other treasures had been confiscated by the police. The warehouse stood empty, open to the wind and dust.

It all began when fifteen-year-old Mateo wanted out of the gang. He was seriously upset after the last robbery, when they had almost killed a security guard. The gang was turning vicious. Mateo wanted no part in killings. They wouldn't listen to Mateo, but they began watching him closely.

When the warehouse was raided, the suspicion of being the snitch fell on Mateo. He had not gone to the police, but he had confided in a friend, Juan Ramon. Mateo told him what he and the gang had been doing. He also told Juan Ramon about the shack at the edge of town where the group slept huddled together after a job. Juan offered to inform the police about the warehouse with an anonymous tip. The raid followed.

Thinking that Mateo was the snitch, the ten waited for a chance to get even. The opportunity came one dark, moonless night. They waylaid Mateo on an empty stretch of the road leading to their shack. They jumped him. Mateo was slashed with a machete and beaten with sticks and pieces of pipe. He was left for dead.

A passing street vendor rattling by with his empty produce cart on his way home that night found Mateo bleeding on the road. He was still alive. The vendor dragged Mateo onto his cart and wheeled him off to the emergency room at St. Theresa Hospital.

Mateo was badly injured. He had suffered a great loss of blood. A machete cut had almost severed his right arm. It took forty-two stitches to close the wound. He had lost part of his little finger on his left hand. His head was a mass of matted hair with wounds oozing blood. His one eye was battered shut. His whole body was one massive bruise with many deep slashes and open welts. The doctors and nurses worked on Mateo for hours. He was given a blood transfusion then stitched and bandaged. He remained unconscious and in intensive care, hanging onto life by a thread. No one knew who he was. The police were called. No clues.

The next day, the story appeared in the daily papers. Juan Ramon read about the attack and suspected the victim might be Mateo. He entered the hospital and strolled through the corridors and wards, mingling with other visitors. He passed the intensive care unit but couldn't recognize the mummy-like wrapped Mateo. Finally, he asked a passing aide if she knew about the victim of last night. She did and pointed out Mateo. Seeing no one around that bed, Juan Ramon stepped slowly closer. As he looked down at Mateo, the one eye fluttered open. After a moment, Mateo recognized Juan Ramon.

In a rasping whisper, Mateo gasped, "They got me!"

Angered, Juan Ramon again informed the police with another anonymous tip, telling them where the ten holed up. All ten were detained that night.

On the day of being transferred to Jalteva, the ten boys were very subdued and scared when they left the detention cell at the jail. They met a much-bandaged Mateo with downcast looks when he was helped from the hospital and aboard the Jalteva bus. Mateo really should not have been released from the hospital yet. His right arm was heavily bandaged and in a sling. His eye, head, and left hand were also still bandaged. His face was all bruises and bright with fever. He was in great pain throughout his bruised and battered body.

The social worker, Mariluz, knew immediately that Mateo could not be taken to Jalteva that day. He had to be kept near a doctor and the hospital for whatever emergency or setback might occur. Jalteva was too far from this help. So instead, she took Mateo to El Hatillo, an observation center in Tegucigalpa. There, she arranged with the nurse for Mateo's care and to get him to the doctor regularly until Mateo healed.

Fifteen days later, Mateo arrived at Jalteva. He was still healing. Around his injured eye, he was sporting all colors of the rainbow. He had not lost his eye, despite the terrible battering it had taken. His right arm and some major cuts were lightly bandaged. He still carried his arm in a sling. The danger of infections setting in had passed. The Jalteva nurse could now tend to the rest of his recovery.

The fifteen days of Mateo's healing at El Hatillo gave the psychologist, the social worker, and Sister Rose time to hold daily sessions with the ten boys individually or in groups. It was a difficult task, leading them through to an understanding of what they had done. Betrayal in a gang could not be forgiven, they firmly believed. What finally convinced them to consider forgiveness was the charge of attempted murder brought against them. The fact that it wasn't Mateo who had snitched to the police about the warehouse or where the boys could be found also helped. However, the ten never did discover that it was Juan Ramon who was responsible for the informing, or that he had only given their location to the police after they had attacked and beaten Mateo and left him for dead.

With Mateo at the center, everyone had to be extra vigilant to make sure that not one of the ten sought revenge. Mateo spent his first weeks in Jalteva in the center's infirmary, making his care easier for the nurse. At the same time, it offered protection for him against any possible reprisal.

When released from the infirmary, Mateo was assigned to a dormitory apart from the other ten. But classes, shop, and other activities with the other boys could still offer opportunities for retaliations, so everyone stayed alert to that possibility.

Later, Mariluz searched for two days in Tegucigalpa for Mateo's mother. She followed clues, visiting the barrio where Mateo had lived before taking to the streets, but she found nothing. She combed the marketplace and the street vendors' stalls. Again, no luck. Finally, she asked Mateo if his mother had any friends who might know where she was.

Mateo replied, "My mother doesn't have any friends."

The mother was never tracked down.

On an outing to Cedros, Mateo disappeared. When it was time to return to the center, nobody could find him. A professor stayed behind to continue the search for a while longer but returned without Mateo. Around suppertime, there was Mateo. Upon being questioned, he said that out of curiosity he had followed a funeral procession down the mountainside to the cemetery hidden away in a vale down below the town. He had gotten distracted by the burial at the grave and had forgotten all about time. When he climbed back up to the park, everyone was gone. He begged bus fare from a lady and caught the last ORME bus of the day back to the turnoff to the center. Then he hiked the two kilometers into Jalteva.

By the end of the year, three of the ten gang members had reached their eighteenth birthdays, so they were released to their families. Being the principal leaders and force behind the group, the tension of possible revenge by the others eased off. Besides, the seven remaining boys had become interested in other things, especially in sports and the theater club.

Mateo still continued to keep a low profile. His scarred body served as a constant reminder to walk softly.

Mateo had chosen the sewing shop as the trade he wanted to prepare for. He showed skill and neatness in his work. Gradually he moved from sewing shirts to sewing pants, and finally to doing the cutting of the cloth for sewing these.

In the classroom, Mateo had a more difficult time. He had never gone to school. The years he had spent abandoned on the streets and running with the gang kept him undernourished and lacking the energy he now needed to study. He joined the first level, which covered the first- and second-grade materials. He had volunteer workers tutoring him on the side, but it was a long, slow process. Many times, Mateo became discouraged. He wanted to quit and just work in the shop, the only thing that brightened his days.

Not being interested in sports, Mateo sauntered into the library one weekend. He took in all the craft projects being worked on by groups of boys under the guidance of orientators and Sister Rose. He watched and waited. Finally, his attention was caught by the trapunto circles on which the sewn outlined figures were being stuffed to make them three-dimensional. He saw the embroidery hoops of different sizes stacked on the table. He asked what they were for.

Sister Rose explained how the circular cloth, once stuffed, would be fitted with a circular backing of a durable fabric. Then the set of cloths would be glued and stretched tightly over and into the hoops. Once taut, the back extra edges would be trimmed off. Next, the front edge of the hoop would be decorated with a suitable lace edging and a colorful ribbon would be placed over the top clamp of the hoop, finishing the art piece. Mateo wanted to try placing the cloths. Soon he became an expert trapunto fitter and decorator.

Mateo also asked who did the sewing around the figures on the trapunto cloth. Then he saw the two sewing machines in the library. He thought he could do that sewing, too. Now he was happily occupied on his weekends. Sometimes when there were lots of trapunto cloths to sew, he worked on these along with his cutter's job in the shop.

Despite Mateo's years of belonging to a gang that survived on the streets by its thievery, he tried to steer clear of this at the center. Once in a while, he failed and snatched some small thing or food in passing.

One day a mysterious "shoestring thief" appeared. Nobody could catch this silent thief. After lights out, sometime during the night, someone was swiping the shoestrings from the other boys' shoes set next to their beds. The boys decided they would take their shoestrings out of their shoes at night and hide them between the sheet and the mattress on which they were sleeping. At last the thief was discovered when Mateo began to negotiate the exchange of packets of shoestrings for candies, fruit, or sweet breads that family visitors had left with their sons.

Mateo never had visitors, so he never had these treats, but he hungered for them. Found out, Mateo admitted what he was doing. He had to learn to respect all things belonging to others. An arrangement was made that he could earn his goodies by offering to do extra jobs. In this way, he picked up *centavos* to buy his own treats without problems.

Mateo discovered a tangerine tree just across the river that separated Jalteva's land from Ramon Mata's property. Mata was Honduras' infamous drug trafficker who had bought his way out of prison. He had guards protecting him and his property. Sometimes Mateo would sneak across the river when all looked clear. He filled his pockets and T-shirt with juicy tangerines, waded back to Jalteva's side, and found a hidden corner to enjoy his harvested loot.

Soon, other boys were going with him. The caper ended when one of the professors was looking for his boys. He found them looting tangerines on the other side of the river. He had to explain the danger of what might happen if one of the armed guards caught them stealing tangerines from Mata's tree. The thought did scare the boys, but they still looked across longingly at the tangerine tree.

Mateo struggled through his first-level studies. He finished the year successfully with average grades, filled with pride that he could now read and write. He moved into the second level, studying the third- and fourth-grade materials. The second year moved along smoothly for him.

Each boy took a turn burning the school waste papers and other garbage in the stone ring down at the edge of the river at the northwest edge of the school grounds. This week was Mateo's turn. He was warned to be sure the fire was completely out or under control before leaving it. All were back in the classroom when a loud whooshing sound and fierce crackling was heard. Smoke was smelled and seen billowing by the river. Everyone rushed out.

A fire was roaring down both sides of the riverbed and through the river brush. It was a huge, beautiful bushfire, rushing along and way out of control. The high flames licked at the edges of the tree branches, searing their leaves and pine needles to a crisp. Boys and personnel rushed in all directions. Buckets and washtubs filled with water from the lagoon were dumped on the creeping flames. Brooms and branches ripped from trees and bushes were used to beat out the running blaze on the grass edge as it rapidly crept toward the school building. After the mad battle, everyone ended up breathless, well-smoked, and sooty. The fire had been beaten to death before it jumped the fence into the fields or across the lawn to the school building.

Mateo just stood there, tears channeling down his sooty face, repeating, "I thought it was out! I'm so sorry! I thought it was out!"

His classroom teacher put his hand on Mateo's shoulder, moving him along with the other boys, saying, "Don't look so beat! I think you'll double-check next time. Just look at the others. They feel like conquering heroes for getting the fire under control. And you helped with that, so feel good about it."

Boys from the streets are used to eating anything wherever they find it. Usually, they have very sturdy stomachs. One day, Mateo found a recently dead dove. He plucked it and roasted it on the sly behind the dormitory. Then he ate it. He got deathly sick. Food poisoning! The nurse tried all possible remedies and managed to get it under control. Mateo survived. After four days, he was up and walking. He was back in classes after being one miserably sick boy.

With the new school year, Mateo moved into the third level, covering the fifth- and sixth-grade materials. He did well, maintaining average grades all year. He graduated. This was quite an achievement for someone who three years before had never gone to school.

Soon Mateo would celebrate his eighteenth birthday. It was time for his final evaluation. His conduct, shop, and classroom efforts were reviewed. He had used his time well while at Jalteva. The problem was where he would go on leaving the center. No mother had been found, despite continuous searches.

Mariluz and Sister Rose helped Mateo work out a plan. A small room was found in the capital in a safe barrio. He could pay his first rents with the shop earnings he had saved over the years. A job was found as a cutter at La Cubana sewing shop. A one-year scholarship was found for him so he could study night school at Instituto Nacional Cultural, where other Jalteva boys were studying. If no scholarship could be found for the second year, Mateo would work that year, save his money, and then continue his studies the following year.

That is what Mateo did. It was tough going. In La Cubana, he was promoted to chief cutter in the central shop with a better salary. His plan of study continued in alternate years—one year studying, one year working—until he completed his high school.

One Saturday evening when returning from work, Mateo cut across the park. There he found one of Jalteva's boys sleeping on a park bench. It was Juan Francisco. He woke the boy and asked him what he was doing there. Juan Francisco said he had just been released last week, but his mother had chased him from their home. She had always rejected him. During his five years at Jalteva, his mother had never visited him nor written to him. She had never agreed to have Juan Francisco home over Christmas and New Year holidays. She didn't want him around. Having never succeeded in finding his own mother, Mateo understood what Juan Francisco was suffering. He invited Juan Francisco to come along to his small room.

Juan Francisco stayed with Mateo. He found work in a mechanic shop. With help from Mariluz and the juvenile court, Juan's mother was ordered to help her son. She still wouldn't have him at home, but she did consent to pay his half of the rent while Juan Francisco lived with Mateo. Later, the two young men went their separate ways, but they both were always willing to help recently released Jalteva boys whenever they found one of them with problems.

Chapter Seven

Roberto

He came handcuffed and under soldier-policeman guard from the central penitentiary. This was Roberto, a tall, lanky boy of sixteen, just skin and bones and filthy dirty. All he had with him were the rags on his back. His face and arms were bruised and scarred with scabs of healing welts. Asked how he got those, Roberto answered that they were from beatings while being questioned by the police and from talking back to a guard.

The first thing for Roberto was getting his lousy locks cropped to the scalp and then a trip to the showers. Next, the nurse checked and treated his bruised body, making notes on the condition in which he had arrived at the center. Roberto's dirty, vermin-ridden clothing was burned. Clean clothing was scavenged from old, unclaimed clothing in the laundry and sewing rooms. Some was borrowed from boys who had extra clothing, lending this until Roberto got his own clothes.

At last, Roberto became the proud owner of two complete sets of clothing, including a pair of solid work shoes. The first day, just after he had labeled his new duds, someone walked off with a pair of his new pants and one of his T-shirts. Roberto immediately reported his loss. In the general formation before lunch, Sister Rose announced the loss. She demanded that the shameless one who took Roberto's possessions please return them at once. Within an hour, Roberto reported back. The stolen items had been returned. He had found them on his bed.

Roberto had a trigger temper that shot off its ugly head for the least cause. He didn't want to be at the center. His spirits frequently fell to a low. In his first interview with the social worker, he was angered at something she said. With a violent sweep of his hand, he knocked everything off her desk to the floor and ran off.

In a session with Sister Rose, Roberto claimed that the whole world was against him. He was defensive, picking constant fights with his companions. It was never his fault that a fight resulted. The other was always to blame.

In his bouts of depression, Roberto disappeared and hid out in some corner or in the fruit groves. Once when his professor was searching for him, he found Roberto in the dorm bathroom with a belt around his neck. He was trying to hang himself from one of the overhead pipes. More counseling was needed with the psychologist!

Jigsaw puzzles always fascinated the boys. They loved looking for the right shape and colors to fit the pieces in their respective places. A puzzle was usually kept on the table in the living area of the dormitory. Anyone could place pieces whenever a moment presented itself. Roberto was good at working on these puzzles, but sometimes he became very possessive. It was HIS castle he was building. Only HE could fit in the castle pieces. If someone else touched it, he became angry. That happened one day. An angry Roberto swept all the pieces into the box lid. He stormed to the door and in one grand sweep tossed all the pieces into the four winds. The lid followed. Then Roberto, fuming, stalked off to bed. Stunned, the other boys begged the professor for his flashlight. They went outside and gathered the lid and as many pieces as they could find in the gravel and grass in front of the dormitory. They didn't find all the pieces, but surprisingly when the puzzle was completed, only five pieces were missing.

Roberto chose the carpenter shop as the trade he wanted to learn. He did quite well with ordinary sawing and hammering but wasn't so lucky when he tried using the electric saw for the first time. He nearly cut off his left thumb. It was slit down to the bone. The ineffective nurse at the time was greener around the gills than Roberto was. When Sister Rose arrived in the infirmary to check on Roberto, the nurse had him standing with his thumb down and bleeding into a dish. Sister quickly turned the thumb upward and got the bleeding stopped with a compress. She tied the thumb against the hand, ready for traveling. With a professor, she got Roberto off to the doctor in Talanga. The doctor, in turn, simply gave Roberto a tetanus shot and sent him off to the hospital in Tegucigalpa.

Finishing at the hospital, the professor took Roberto to his home. His father's woman companion went into hysterics and almost fainted when she saw the bloodied bandage. By staying with his father and her, Roberto's father could take him to the doctor for regular checkups for his thumb. When it was healed, he could return to Jalteva. In a week, Roberto was back at the center. His thumb was healing well. No infection had set in, but it was still one very sore thumb.

Not being able to work in the shop for a while, Roberto spent more time in the library. He did extra studying of his third-level materials and did extra reading. The librarian guided him to books that might help him toward anger control.

The date for the monthly birthday celebration was set. This month, Roberto would be celebrating his seventeenth birthday. A special table was set with tablecloths and flowers. The birthday boys and personnel were served here. A huge slice of birthday cake was their dessert. Each boy received a wrapped birthday gift. They all loved this.

However, another tradition wasn't so pleasant. Sneaking up behind the birthday guests, other boys "baptized" them by dumping buckets of water over each head. Roberto came up sputtering, furious that he was soaked and dripping. His anger almost rocked the celebration to a halt. Seeing the other wet boys and personnel laughing, shaking off water, and wringing out shirts, Roberto joined in the laughter. At least his piece of cake and his gift weren't drenched.

During the monthly dormitory inventory checkup and the review of each boy's locker and belongings, it was discovered that a number of bed sheets were missing. The orientators in charge became more vigilant, watching especially the few possible suspects. Roberto was one of these. He was seen coming out of the thorn brush from the direction of Tablon, the small village set among the rocks just a ten-minute walk from Jalteva.

The professor followed Roberto. He met up with two other boys. The three stealthily wove their way through the mango grove up to the old silo in the off-limits area. The professor watched Roberto divide the loot—candy, sweet breads, and cigarettes. Next, from a wrapping of newspaper, Roberto pulled out a square of "dulce"—a solid block of crude brown sugar. From under a bush, one of the boys dragged a five-gallon lard can. It was filled with cut-up pieces of raw squash in water. Roberto shaved strips of "dulce" from the sugar block into the can. Meanwhile, the other two lit a fire prepared with a circle of stones. The three sat around the fire, watching the squash boil and leaning back to enjoy a smoke.

When the sugar was melted into the squash and the pulp was well-cooked, the professor made his presence known. The three startled culprits jumped up in shocked surprise. The professor geared his direct question to Roberto, asking him how many sheets he had sold to acquire such an amount of goods. Caught, Roberto answered that he had sold two bed sheets. The other two boys, when questioned, had to admit to having taken a turn selling bed sheets, too, at different times.

Then came the unpleasant part. The cigarettes and matches were confiscated. The sweet breads, candy, and the can of cooked squash were carried down to the younger boys' dormitory where the culprits had to serve their goodies to these boys. It almost killed the three to watch these little guys gobble up their goodies.

The final humiliation came when the professor and the center's subdirector took the three culprits back to Tablon. The first stop was at the police delegation. A sergeant went with them to the store pointed out as the trading post. When accused of having bartered things for bed sheets, the startled woman denied this at first.

Finally, with threats of a house search and jail time from the sergeant and three pairs of accusing eyes glaring at her, she admitted to having done the deal. The sergeant ordered her to return the bed sheets. She reluctantly did so. What a surprise though, when she handed over eight bed sheets instead of just the two they were expecting! The sergeant left her with the additional threat that if she continued to trade with Jalteva boys, she would be arrested for contributing to theft on the part of juveniles. She did not demand the value of the items traded for sheets.

Getting to know more about Roberto each day helped in understanding him better. While telling the story of his childhood to Sister Rose, he said he had been abandoned by his mother. She had left him on a seat in his father's bus while he was in the cantina drinking and getting drunk with his friends. When the staggering man returned to his bus, he found a very red-faced, furiously squalling infant with a very wet diaper. The child had kicked off his thick blanket.

Taking the child, the father returned to the cantina to consult with his friends. The child was passed from one set of drunken arms to the next, each man trying to quiet the crying of the infant. One drunk, in a moment of lucidity, thought maybe it was the wet diaper that was annoying the child. He asked the bartender for a towel, and a none-too-clean one was handed across. Soon the drunk had it replacing the wet diaper. The baby continued to squall but in a less angry tone. Hiccupped sobs broke through. The bartender finally suggested that the child might be hungry. He took a napkin, soaked a corner in sugar water, and gave it to the baby to suck on. The child quieted and lay contented on the bar.

Roberto spent his entire childhood being passed into the care of one woman after the other—all friends of his father—while his father was away driving his bus. Sometimes the bus followed a very erratic course as it was driven down the road. Drunk or not, Roberto's father never beat him or his women friends.

Holy Week arrived and the traditions opened a week of baking, so that each boy could enjoy an Easter nest with a variety of cookies and candies. Roberto eagerly lent his hands in tirelessly making hundreds of cookie dough balls. He liked the reward at the end of each day's baking—two cookies from each recipe baked, and a bag of cookie crumbs from broken cookies and the baking sheets.

One Good Friday during the Way of the Cross in the liturgical celebration, someone pushed Roberto. In anger, he erupted into a burst of gross, threatening insults, bringing the liturgy to an abrupt halt. Seething, he left the group, stalking off towards the lagoon. One of the professors went after him and talked him into coming back. He sat a little apart from the other boys and stayed quiet but remained in a very sullen mood throughout the rest of the ceremony. At least, the solemn liturgy ended peacefully. Roberto even joined in the Veneration of the Cross.

When Mother's Day came around, Roberto never had a mother to celebrate with him at the center. His father never came to visit, either. Nor did anyone ever write to him. Seeing the joy of the other boys with their mothers and families always left Roberto sad. He hid away in a corner of the library for most of the day. A few of the other motherless boys sometimes joined him, each commiserating with the other.

Sister Rose spent extra time with them, talking and trying to cheer them up. She wanted them to know that somewhere they each had a mother to whom they should be most grateful for having given them life. Together they said a prayer for their mothers, asking God's blessing on them wherever they might be. Sister set up table games and brought special snacks along as prizes for the winners. This eased their sadness a bit in their motherless world.

Having celebrated his eighteenth birthday, Roberto had to leave the center. He had graduated from primary school, learned the carpentry trade, and learned to keep his anger under control more frequently. He was a less angry boy. He felt he could make it on his own. He didn't want to go to a regular high school but was interested in bettering his trade, becoming a professional master carpenter. Exploring the possibilities, a scholarship was found with a bank. This would for pay his four six-month courses at INFOP, an industrial trade school in Tegucigalpa.

When the juvenile court approved Roberto's release from Jalteva, he returned home to live with his drunken father and his father's women friends. Roberto's father tacked a small room addition onto the back of the shack, where Roberto could be by himself. This room was his. He studied hard, keeping his scholarship. Completing each six-month course at INFOP, Roberto proudly showed off his certificates. At the end of two years, he graduated as a master carpenter, and made a special frame for his diploma.

His father helped him set up and equip his own carpenter shop in a corner of the Mayoreo General Market in upper Comayaguela. Working hard, Roberto began producing beautiful furniture, which he sold right there in the marketplace. Sometimes larger furniture stores commissioned special pieces of furniture from Roberto. He proved to be a true master carpenter and took in apprentices to teach them the trade he so loved.

Chapter Eight

Tomas

The uphill, narrow, red-clay road was lined on either side with cantinas. The battered wooden benches outside of each were crowded with red-faced drunks, clutching tightly their bottles of favorite alcoholic drinks. Bloodshot eyes followed the old and young women passing by, punctuated by exclamations of, "Ay, que linda!" (Oh, how beautiful!) The road climbed steeply up the mountainside, devoid of all vegetation—not a tree or bush in sight. It led up to a desolate barrio, El Pastel. Dilapidated shacks, tucked away among scattered rocks, leaned into one another along the rugged paths winding around the makeshift homes.

Looking at the view of the city, one could see the general cemetery below. The closely packed tombstones and mausoleums contrasted sharply with tall weeds, grasses, and trees surrounding the many graves. The cemetery stretched down the incline to the San Isidro Market and the Choluteca River bed. Having no play area, the barrio children jumped the crumbling cemetery wall and played hide-and-seek among the tombs, high jumping from some, and having a great time until chased by the guard at the main gate. The children were especially interested in the hanging edges just above the river, where rains exposed tombs by washing away soil and even human bones into the river.

Tomas was found playing here. The cemetery was his playground. He lived above in El Pastel. His family had moved there from the northern coast when his father was employed as a parking lot gatekeeper at the Education Ministry, located on the other side of the market and the river. Tomas and his four younger brothers were cared for by their mother. Tomas was eleven years old, and the youngest brother was eight months old.

One day, tragedy struck. A policeman was chasing a fleeing market thief and shooting wildly. One of his stray bullets penetrated Tomas' home. It struck his mother dead where she stood. Screaming children brought the neighbors running. They found the mother lying in a pool of blood where she had fallen.

Now Tomas' playground was no longer a playground. It was the burial place for his mother. The fun went out of his life. He became rebellious and refused to go to school. He would not obey the woman his father hired to care for the children while he was at work. Sometimes Tomas' father took him along to work, but the boy often disappeared into the marketplace, where he swiped things and angry vendors chased him, shouting for the police.

Finally, as the situation worsened, Tomas' father consulted with the juvenile court. Tomas was considered a "social risk." The judge sent him to Jalteva as a preventive measure. At the center,

Tomas was lost and miserable. He missed his family, especially his mother. He needed lots of love and a hug once in a while.

Tomas had completed his second grade, so he entered the second level, studying third- and fourth-grade materials. He heard the musical group playing, and the drums especially impressed him. He wanted to be part of that. He was assigned one hour to practice the drums in the music shop. The other two shop hours he spent in the gardening shop. He learned to plant seedbeds, to prepare the soil, to transplant, and to care for his garden plot. He liked it when his labors began to produce. After supplying the kitchen and selling in the market, he could enjoy carrots, tomatoes, and even cantaloupe during his morning breaks. He sometimes stashed a few of these vegetables in his pockets for afternoon or evening snacks.

Tomas enjoyed the central grass plaza at the center. It was edged with tall African date-palm trees. These reminded him of his earlier years of living on the coast. He climbed these to reach the tempting, red-orange fruit clustered at the base of the palm fronds. Because it was never hot or dry enough at Jalteva, the dates never matured. They did produce the pit, which remained an oily nut. Tomas loved to eat these overly rich bits.

One day while at the top, Tomas slipped and skidded down over the spiky stubs left from cutting off the branches as they died and dried. These stubs sliced into his chest, arms, and thighs, leaving his exposed skin filled with spiny-edged slivers. The nurse had quite the task to carefully remove these prickly bits with tweezers and then get him all doctored up. He was one suffering lad for a few days.

Longing to see his family, Tomas ran away one day with two of the boys from his dormitory and an older boy, Miguel. Arriving in Talanga, Miguel stole a car and drove the four of them in style to Tegucigalpa. They were stopped at the entrance to the city and caught. Miguel didn't have a driver's license nor any identification. The juvenile court soon had the four boys brought back to Jalteva.

Tomas wasn't happy with the sanction he received on his return. He was angry with the director. On the sly, Tomas took fine splinters of wood and stuffed these into the locks on the director's bedroom and office doors, jamming the mechanisms. When the director tired to put his key in, it wouldn't enter. Examining the lock, the director discovered the tiny pieces of wood blocking it.

It took the carpenter shop master quite a while to clear the splinters from both locks. Suspecting Tomas, the director asked him why he had done this. Tomas' only answer was he didn't like the director. After a good talk with the director, Tomas accepted his first sanction, plus an additional one for jamming the locks. Now instead of helping to clean the corridors, Tomas had to clean them alone.

When the rains flooded down from the mountains, the strong river currents washed out the dike in the upper river. This emptied the water for irrigation in the storage pool held behind the dike. All the boys and personnel were part of the rebuilding of the structure. They worked in shifts. A gravel truck was rented to haul in the loads of sand and gravel. As one load of gravel was brought in, Tomas rode on top with a few other boys. He entertained himself by tossing stones at the telephone poles as the truck sped past. Flinging a larger stone, Tomas missed the post. His stone bounced onto the windshield of a village bus coming in the opposite direction toward the truck. The glass shattered, scattering flying pieces over the driver and passengers.

The bus stopped. The truck stopped. The bus driver jumped off the bus, waving a huge pistol. He ordered all his passengers off the bus and in a line across the road so the truck couldn't move on. Nobody argued with the gun-waving driver. After a heated discussion with the truck driver and fierce glares at the boys on top of the load, the bus driver let his passengers scramble back onto the bus. With his gun pointed out the window, he followed the truck to the center. There, more discussion followed. The administrator paid L. 500 ($250) for replacing the windshield. That had been one expensive stone.

One morning, Tomas overslept. As a result, he was grumpy and late for the morning prayer and breakfast formation. His sanction was to jog five times around the grassy plaza before entering to eat his breakfast. Tomas refused to do so and stomped off to his dormitory, sacrificing his breakfast in anger and self-pity.

The bell rang for shop. It was a blistering hot day. Tomas went off to his garden plot, still very angry and very hungry, although he wouldn't admit it. He scrounged around for some vegetables to eat but found only weeds. He hoed away furiously, weeding his new plants. Sweat soaked through his shirt and dripped off his face. The sun blazed down hotter still.

Without any warning, Tomas keeled over and sprawled in the dirt in a dead faint. He had suffered heatstroke. The shop master and some of the boys rushed over, one boy bringing his wheelbarrow with him. Unceremoniously, the boys picked Tomas up and plunked him into the wheelbarrow. Another boy dumped a gallon of water over his hot face. At a run, the new "ambulance" service pushed off for the infirmary. It took the nurse a while to cool Tomas down while two boys held him upright in the shower. The "ambulance" driver told the nurse that Tomas had refused to jog around the plaza that morning and had stalked off to the dormitory without eating breakfast. The nurse dried off Tomas and got him into a pair of muslin pajamas.

Once he was settled on a cot, she prepared a bowl of Maggi chicken soup for him. When Tomas had recovered sufficiently, the nurse served the soup with packets of saltine crackers to Tomas. He gulped the soup in quick slurps. Cracker after cracker disappeared in crackling crunches. With his hunger satisfied, Tomas lay back on the cot, relaxed, and dozed off. By noon, he was up and in line for dinner, not willing to risk being assigned another jog around the plaza or going hungry again.

Besides music, Tomas loved to dramatize. He joined the theater club. He practiced short parts in the presentations. One of these was a modern-day parable, *The Saga of the Wounded Bird.* It was the story of a bird with a broken wing seeking shelter among the trees in the forest. The forest was made up of a group of boys standing backstage with hands joined and swaying rhythmically. They murmured softy as the wind moved through the trees. At center stage, a group of boys formed a sturdy oak tree, standing in a circle back-to-back with their strong arms stretched out before them. Another group formed a weeping willow, with arms drooping gracefully downward toward the ground. A third group formed a rugged spruce tree, standing tall, facing inward, and with arms curving outward and hands stretched forward like branches of an evergreen.

A narrator told the story. Along limped the bird, clutching its broken wing. It begged shelter of the oak tree. The oak gruffly refused, wanting nothing to do with the injured bird. So the bird hobbled on to the weeping willow. Again, the bird begged for shelter. The arrogant willow refused in a fastidious voice filled with haughtiness, wanting nothing sickly or wounded to touch its delicate, lacy branches. Sadly, the bird trudged tiredly on to the spruce, begging for shelter once more. The spruce opened and pulled the wounded bird into its circle of branches.

During the narration and the action, Tomas played his first dramatic role. He stood at the edge of the swaying forest with his arms raised high in front of him in a connecting circle. A huge grin covered his dark, happy face, showing a gleaming row of white teeth. Shining down on the entire scene, Tomas was the sun.

Standing in the corner of the dorm's living area was the professor's beautiful, ten-speed bike. It was very tempting for Tomas. Finally, one day when no one was around, Tomas could no longer resist the lure of the bike. He would try just a few rounds right there, circling the living area inside the dorm.

Tomas took off, slowly building up speed. On the fifth round, he curved too closely to the front windows. One handle bar clipped the edge of the window frame and Tomas was flung into the windows. The glass shattered. So did Tomas' left arm. Glass sliced a few deep cuts into his forearm and elbow. The bike clattered to the ground and skidded into the corner.

The crash and Tomas' howl of pain brought professors to investigate. Seeing Tomas in a bloodied heap, they rushed forward. Carefully, they turned Tomas over. He had passed out from the pain and the shock. One professor sent a boy for the director. Another boy was sent for the truck driver. Two of the professors prepared Tomas' arm for travel. It was wrapped in a towel and tied to his chest. Director and driver arrived at the scene at the same time.

Tomas was off to the hospital in Tegucigalpa. There, the doctor stitched the deep cuts and bandaged them. After setting the bones, the doctor put on a half-cast under the damaged forearm to give easy access to bandage changes. A wide elastic bandage was wound tightly around the entire arm to hold everything in place. Tomas returned to the center with his arm cradled in a sling. There was no sanction given. The bike had not been damaged and Tomas was suffering enough.

On All Souls' Day, the boys were gathered in the main hall with Sister Rose for a special prayer service for everyone's deceased relatives and friends. In the middle of the solemnity, a big, fat hen strutted across the stage. She clucked her way to the cupboard where the musical instruments were stored. There she settled comfortably on top of it. The eyes of Jalteva were upon her.

The minute the celebration ended, Tomas and other boys raced across the stage and slammed into the cupboard with a bang. The poor hen was badly upset and took off in a flurry of wings. She hadn't even had time to lay an egg. She was so startled and shaken up that she probably wouldn't lay another egg for a week. The way Tomas had hit the cupboard, it sounded like he had broken his other arm.

Questioning the "why" for the stampede to the cupboard, it was discovered that there was an egg racket in progress. The price of eggs had shot up sky high and the administrator wasn't buying more than a carton of eggs a week. As a result, the boys were hunting eggs. They watched and checked where the free-running hens were laying their eggs. For each egg found and handed in to the cooks, a boy received a bun, a cookie, or a banana—something to eat in exchange for the egg. The boys, in their diligent search for eggs, kept the hens in a state of nervous prostration.

Three years sped by. Tomas had become an excellent horticulturist. He had completed his primary school education. Soon he would be fifteen years old. When agricultural engineers came to the center to give courses to the boys, one of them, Don Elias, noted how skilled Tomas was in the field. He offered Tomas a scholarship at the John F. Kennedy Agricultural School in Atlantida if he was interested. He would have to board at the school. The courses would last three years, but he would graduate as an agricultural specialist in the branch of agriculture he chose.

Tomas was interested. His father approved the plan and was happy for his son. Despite the fact that he would be away from home for another three years, Tomas would be returning to the coastal area where he had been born. He accepted the scholarship. The juvenile court approved the plan and released Tomas from Jalteva.

The social worker helped Tomas gather all the documents and papers he needed for entering the school. His father supplied all the clothing and personal items required of Tomas while studying. In January, Tomas was off to the John F. Kennedy Agricultural School.

Tomas worked and studied hard at the school. He specialized in the raising of coffee. Graduating with honors, Don Elias helped Tomas find a good-paying job at the Ministry of Natural Resources as a technician in the coffee industry. He traveled to the coffee plantations throughout the country, teaching new techniques and supervising the *beneficios*, the plants where coffee was prepared for the market.

Tomas lived simply. He saved his money, putting it into a savings account. After hard work for five years, Tomas began searching for the woman with whom he wanted to share his life. He found her. Her name was Margarita. She was a secretary at the central office of the Natural Resources Ministry. They dated regularly for a year and then decided to marry once they found a home. Hearing of this, an elderly friend, Don Julio, sold them his home in Colonia Miraflores at a very reasonable price.

The marriage was blessed with five children. Shortly after the birth of the fifth child, Margarita became ill. It was leukemia. She lingered and weakened over a period of six months and suddenly died. For his children, it was a repetition of Tomas' own childhood. Now, like his father, he had to forge on alone.

Chapter Nine

Raul

Raul was just another of the many twelve-year-olds wandering in the city streets of Tegucigalpa. He was one of the lost youngsters, begging for food or swiping it from any of the many baskets cluttering the walkways between the market stalls. He slept wherever he found a protective street corner, lying on spread cardboard cartons, curled up with his back to the wind.

No one knew from where Raul had originated. He himself couldn't say where his mother now lived. He only remembered that they had migrated from one poor hovel to another on the outskirts of villages in southern Honduras.

Despite his vagabonding life, Raul remained healthy. His sturdy body was small in build. He was a bright-eyed, mischievous boy. He loved running and playing soccer, easily joining any group of street boys in spontaneous games. Most of the time, it was simply barefoot racing across empty lots, kicking around tin cans or a tattered ball of tightly rolled rags. On rare occasions, someone miraculously produced a battered, well-used soccer ball. Then, what joy for Raul to kick aloft the ball in a high arc. He loved controlling the ball, swiftly moving it downfield toward the two stones which marked the goal. Raul's aim was deceptive. The goalie was often caught off guard when Raul slammed the ball through the goal with a fast, exact kick in an unexpected spot.

When social workers from the welfare organization known as the Junta began gathering boys from the streets, Raul was one of the boys picked up. At the time, a juvenile court did not exist in Honduras, but Jalteva did. It was an agricultural center for sheltering poor, abandoned, or vagabonding boys. Here they could work in agriculture or learn a trade. They could even go to the small primary school for a more formal education if they wished.

Always ready for a new adventure, Raul agreed to go to Jalteva. His papers were prepared. He knew his birth date. His birth certificate was found in the city hall register. Only a mother was named. She had given birth to Raul in Choluteca with a midwife assisting. The mother couldn't be traced. No other relatives responded either to numerous radio calls describing Raul.

When Raul arrived at Jalteva, it was just an agricultural school with 180 boys being cared for. The personnel was made up of young primary school teachers and shop masters, men who were interested in educating and working with neglected boys. These men carried the full program from 5:00 A.M. until 9:00 P.M.—classes, shop, farming, and sports. On some days, boys and personnel arose at 4:00 A.M. They jogged for an hour from the main entrance, across a creek, and finally along the village edge of Tablon, back to the entrance of Jalteva. That really got everyone's blood circulating, and all were wide awake for beginning a new day.

Raul entered full tilt into the activities at the center. He started his formal education in first grade. Reading became his first love. This occupied many of his hours once he recognized words and meanings. Picture books with a few written lines were quickly devoured.

Then Raul became fascinated by Indians, moving from easy reading books to more difficult ones on the subject. When no more Indian stories surfaced for Raul, he asked the librarian, Miguel, where he could find more. Miguel used the opportunity to interest Raul in other topics—adventure, mysteries, and such. Raul thought mysteries might intrigue him. Soon he was reading a wide variety of other stories, but always hoping he would find one more new Indian story.

Raul chose the carpenter shop as the trade he wished to learn. He was very skilled in handling wood and the equipment. He took great pride in making chests of drawers, tables, and even headboards for beds. His favorite craftsmanship was that of making small wooden toys for children. These were given to the children of Jalteva's workers on Children's Day or at Christmastime.

Jalteva had a small zoo set in one corner between the coffee plants along a ravine and the mango orchard next to the lagoon. There were three monkeys among the various animals. One of these was Panchita. She was clever and somehow could snap links on a long chain fastened to her collar. The chain permitted her to climb and swing through the many branches of the large tree that was her home. Sometimes, though, she wanted to roam and explore farther afield. Whenever she escaped, she wreaked havoc in the kitchen storerooms. It was always difficult to recapture her because she leaped from one metal ceiling beam to the other in the storerooms, kitchen, and main hall.

On one of her escapes, Panchita took to "kit"-napping. She snatched one of the newborn kittens from a litter in the corner of the back storeroom. For three days she cuddled the poor kitty, always managing to escape anyone trying to snatch the dangling piece of chain still attached to her collar.

Raul joined a group giving chase after Panchita. He ran across the roof of the main hall, which also served as cafeteria. He almost caught Panchita, but as he stepped onto one roof panel at the highest point, his foot smashed through, bringing the entire panel down and Raul with it. With a tremendous clatter, debris and Raul plunged down, landing on a cafeteria table below. It served as a trampoline, but the plywood table top shattered. The entire table collapsed. Everyone thought Raul was done for, but he was only stunned and just suffered a twisted ankle.

Meanwhile, Panchita stashed the kitty in an eave spout where one of the boys found it and returned the bedraggled creature to its litter, more dead than alive. When Panchita returned for the kitty, it was gone. Searching and not finding it, Panchita returned to the litter. There, greatly enraged, she chattered furiously at the mother cat, now standing guard with humped back and raised hackles, hissing at Panchita. Getting too close, the cat swiped Panchita across the nose with a clawed paw. This sent Panchita to the beams, wildly screeching in fury. After another long chase, minus Raul, Panchita was finally captured. The boys got a very exhausted monkey, with a sore nose, fastened to a new, stronger chain and back into her tree. There Panchita sat on a leafless limb, quiet and looking very disconsolate.

With colder weather and the hurricane season blowing strong winds over Honduras, it became kite-flying time for the boys. With other boys, Raul always made a huge colorful kite. Thin bamboo tubes supported his framework. Over this, multicolored tissue paper was glued in decorative patterns. A long-ribboned crepe paper tail was added. Attaching the spooled cord readied the kite for flight. Raul ran gleefully across the soccer fields, releasing his kite into the winds. He spent many hours of his free time with his kite, until one day, a stronger wind snapped the cord and away sailed Raul's beautiful kite.

Soccer, of course, was Raul's favorite sport. Short in stature, he held his own while playing with taller boys. His swift running and agile footwork won him a place on the center's official soccer team. He always played barefooted, feeling clumsy when his feet were confined in soccer shoes.

The puppet theater became another of Raul's interests. He loved the humor and mischief he could present in his acts. In the carpenter shop, he helped make the three-paneled stage with its open central window. When his classroom professor designed and drew the folklore scenes on the panels, Raul helped paint these and did the final varnishing. He also made the stools needed for the actors to sit on while manipulating the puppets in the stage window. He helped select the dramatizations and plan the shows. Sometimes he even invented his own humorous dialogues. He loved taking the role of master of ceremonies with a clown puppet. In this role, he carried on with clever jokes and humor to connect the different acts being presented.

Part of a puppeteer's job was to create the needed puppet characters. Raul came up with a brilliant idea: have each of the 180 boys at the center make one puppet. It became a month-long project. Each classroom, in turn, prepared fine paper strips from magazine pages or newspapers. These were soaked in water overnight. The cooks made the homemade paste for each group and papier-mâché was in the making. Each boy formed a puppet head around a modified, finger-width toilet paper roll. Talk about creativity! Each classroom took on the look of a headhunter's lodge with puppet heads lined up on the windowsills to dry thoroughly. At the end of the month, all the heads were painted. The puppeteers then selected the characters needed for their shows.

Next, the art room was turned topsy-turvy while the boys searched for remnants of colorful cloth suitable for the puppets' dress. Sister Rose bought extra cloth sold in bargain bundles in stores. The sewing shop had the honor of making all the costumes for the puppets. The results were fantastic—witches, magicians, clowns, bandits, soldiers, old men and women, youngsters—everything one could think of emerged.

With all the rest of the puppets on display, the boys belonging to the puppet theater club could select their own six or eight puppets if they planned to set up their own puppet show in their barrio when they left the center. Raul selected eight puppets for his future shows and stored them in the art room. Other puppets were packaged in packets of six to a set. These were held until Children's Day. Then, a packet was given on that day to each of the fifteen primary schools in the area. The remaining puppets were sold in the annual craft sale in December.

Raul also loved to sing. He joined the center's chorus and was faithful in coming to the Saturday evening rehearsals. On many occasions, Jalteva's chorus was invited to sing at celebrations. One such was the twenty-first anniversary of the founding of the Junta, on March 28. The chorus, the puppeteers, and the musical *conjunto* were all asked to perform in the open-air show being held in the Central Morazán Plaza in Tegucigalpa in front of the San Miguel Cathedral, where a temporary stage had been set up.

The first necessity was finding an electrical outlet for the sound amplifiers and the electric guitars. A soldier helped the boys find one in the subterranean tunnel leading to the underground restrooms. When a TV sound truck arrived, a cable was extended all the way up to the stage for the microphones.

The show was scheduled to begin at 6:00 P.M. but didn't get underway until 7:20 P.M. The puppet show, with Raul as master of ceremonies, was the first of Jalteva's group to perform. It became the star of the evening. The puppeteers outdid themselves in cleverness and running comedy—fine showmanship.

Two numbers before Jalteva's chorus was to sing with the electric guitar accompaniment, someone ripped out a cable connection and walked off with it. No more sound for the guitars! The television emcee for the entire show skipped over the Jalteva chorus and announced as the closing act a frog-voiced group—each singer trilling off in his own croaking version of the song. Sister Rose and the Jalteva boys jumped the announcer, but he was too flustered to correct his error. Raul grabbed his microphone and announced three of Jalteva's songs, which could be sung without a guitar. The chorus did well and closed the show at 9:30 P.M. to a great round of applause.

With people milling about, the boys packed up all the instruments and the puppet theater, loading everything onto Jalteva's truck. Then everyone still had to eat. A surprising, near-miracle was that the Junta had given each boy L. 3.50 ($1.75)—something that had never happened before. The startled owner of a nearby snack bar stood open-mouthed when twenty-two boys descended upon him at 10:00 P.M. like a swarm of hungry locusts. The boys literally wiped clean his establishment.

It was midnight by the time the boys reached the center.

September arrived. Now after six years at Jalteva, Raul had completed his primary education and was ready for high school. He had become a good carpenter, skilled in producing neat, beautiful furniture. He had celebrated his eighteenth birthday. His time was up at Jalteva. It was an unsettling moment for Raul because despite another radio call, no one had responded to it. Where would Raul go? Where would he live?

One of the professors at the center from nearby Cedros, Professor Martin, had been Raul's baptismal godfather just the week before. Raul had made his First Holy Communion and was confirmed on that same day with fifteen other boys. Martin solved Raul's problem. He offered to be responsible for him. Raul could live in a small storage building just across the road from Martin's home and store. Martin had no children of his own, just an adopted daughter. He would consider Raul as a son, being responsible for his living expenses. A Stateside St. Vincent de Paul Conference offered a scholarship that would take care of Raul's high school studies at Instituto Alma Latina in Cedros. In his spare time, Raul could help out in the store or work in the carpentry shop of Martin's brother-in-law. The small salary he earned would cover his personal needs.

The plan moved ahead. Evaluations were sent to the now-existing juvenile court. Approval was given. Raul was all set to begin his new independent life in Cedros.

After siesta on September 14, Raul stopped off at Sister Rose's office to share more of his dreams. He was still short and stocky because he had never grown much in height while at the center. He was eager and vibrant, excited about his planned life for the future. Before leaving the office, Raul asked Sister if he could go along with the musical *conjunto* to Orica. The boys were going to play at the master carpenter's wedding that evening. Being one of the carpenter's students, Raul hoped to take part in the celebration. Sister advised Raul to ask the director for permission. Maybe he would permit Raul to go along. Raul asked and permission was granted.

Around 3:00 P.M., Jalteva's truck and another flatbed truck, loaded with boys and instruments, took off for Orica. Fifteen minutes later, Sister Rose heard a truck's motor grinding away from the kitchen area. She stood up to see a white pickup truck rounding the corner of the main hall. It was the truck of an El Guante neighbor, Don Rafael. He was driving slowly toward her office. She moved into the corridor to see what visitors he was bringing.

The truck didn't stop. It continued slowly toward the infirmary area. Then Sister recognized Professor Martin and *conjunto* boys huddled around someone lying flat in the bed of the truck. She rushed up the corridor to the infirmary in time to see the professor and some of the boys carrying someone into the infirmary. Moving into the examining room, Sister saw Raul lying so still on the gurney. He didn't seem to be breathing. The nurse was working over him frantically, but there was no response of any kind, no sign of life.

In shock, Sister Rose asked, "What happened? I was just talking to him a few minutes ago!"

Uncomprehending, the once happy group, off to a wedding, had returned in tears with a broken body. Professor Martin, in tears also, explained. The flatbed truck he had been driving hit a deep pothole about a quarter of a mile down the rugged, unpaved main highway. The impact had bounced Raul high into the air and tossed him like a rag doll right off the moving truck. He was slammed into the road. He was killed instantly. The back of his skull was crushed, and both his neck and back were broken. This precious young man-boy of eighteen now lay dead. His bright eyes were closed and his handsome face was stilled forever.

Again, radio calls went out. Again, as so many times before, no response from family or anyone.

The nurse and the director prepared the body. Raul was laid out in a simple, mahogany-stained, pine coffin which he himself had helped build in his shop classes. His companions now had helped Sister Rose line it with tacked-in white crepe paper.

When all was ready, boys from Raul's class carefully carried the coffin to the main hall where it was balanced on two chairs. Other boys brought in hurriedly made laurel and flower wreaths. All the boys and personnel gathered. Sister Rose led a special service of prayer and song. This began the all-night vigil. Boys came and went. Some prayed. Some sang. Others just sat in silence. They were remembering a deeply loved friend.

Since embalming wasn't done, burial would take place in Cedros within twenty-four hours on September 15, Honduras' Independence Day. Professor Martin had made all the arrangements, giving place on his own cemetery plot for Raul. Padre Humberto Rivera would celebrate the funeral Mass.

The next morning, all Independence Day and civic celebrations were canceled at the center and in Cedros, where Raul was well-known. Jalteva's entire staff and all 180 boys climbed aboard three cargo trucks and an ORME bus from Cedros, plus other cars and pickup trucks lent for the day. The same white pickup truck driven again by Don Rafael now carried Raul's coffin piled high with laurel and flower wreaths. His classmates rode along with the coffin as it led a dusty caravan moving solemnly off on the half-hour drive to Cedros.

Arriving in Cedros, the entire village was there to meet the funeral cortege. The high school students formed an honor guard as the coffin was carried into the church. They then joined the Jalteva boys in the packed church of "El Señor del Buen Fin." More wreaths and flowers were piled on the closed casket. Padre Rivera celebrated the Requiem Mass. The Jalteva boys sang beautifully. Raul's First Communion class all received Communion again, this time without him.

After Mass, Jalteva boys and Cedros high school boys alternated turns carrying the coffin on their shoulders down the steep mountain path to the cemetery in the hollow below. Midway down at the primary school, the procession stopped and another wake was held. All the school children paid their respects and joined in the prayers and songs. Then the procession moved on. Raul was laid to rest in the dug grave. With more songs, the boys and high school students manning the shovels in shifts filled in the grave. When completed, the wreaths and flowers carried along were piled high on the mound of raw earth.

Everyone stood around for a while after the burial. All were remembering this friendly, happy, curious, adventuresome, fun-loving, lively boy. Plans had been changed by the mysterious workings of a God whose ways are sometimes very hard to understand—God's ways which carry some deeper message for those who are left behind.

Two weeks after Raul's funeral, the most astonishing event took place. A Jeep from the Junta headquarters arrived at the center. Along with Dona Zoe, the head of the rehabilitation department, a tiny, sunburned woman with unkempt graying hair got out of the car. She was dressed in a long, faded, flower-patterned skirt and a green and yellow-striped, well-worn blouse. She wore pink shower slippers on her feet. In her hands she clutched a plastic bag. Descriptive words screamed "poor" and "pathetic." She was very nervous and unsure of herself. She was introduced as Dona Marta, Raul's mother! Stunned, everyone expressed sympathy, despite the fact that she had not connected with her son for more than six years.

After dinner, the director and Dona Zoe took Dona Marta to the cemetery in Cedros to visit Raul's grave. On returning to the center, Dona Marta explained that she had really come to the center to claim the money Raul had earned while at the center. With gasps of surprise, everyone stood in shocked silence. Incredible!

It was calmly explained to her that Raul hadn't earned any money while at Jalteva. The center had sheltered and educated her son for six years and now had buried him because she had never claimed him as her son. The personnel and boys of Jalteva had been his family. Disappointed, Dona Marta broke into tears for the first time. She had so hoped to reap some economic aid on this visit.

However, Dona Zoe did not abandon Dona Marta to her unhappy fate. She traveled south with her and saw with her own eyes the miserable dugout home in the hillside, covered over with scraps of tin, plastic pieces, and thick cardboards. It was a place unfit even for animals. Here Dona Marta struggled to make a pitiful life for her four other children. Dona Zoe helped move the family to a shelter in Choluteca. A small house was found in a barrio on the edge of the city. The Junta settled a six-month pension on Dona Marta to help her furnish and settle into the new home. A job was found for her as a domestic servant in a city household.

As for Raul, he wasn't forgotten. During the two weeks following his burial, the masonry shop built a tiled mausoleum over his grave. The soldering shop crafted a delicately designed metal cross that was cemented at the head of the tomb. It bore his name, date of birth, and date of death.

Every year on All Souls' Day, a group of boys still goes to Cedros with Sister Rose to clear the weeds and rubbish from around the grave, hold a prayer service, and smother the site with flower wreaths. His Jalteva family will never forget him.

Chapter Ten

Carlos

A heavy deluge of rain was falling as a mud-covered Jeep pulled up to the main entrance of Jalteva. At the gatehouse, passengers scrambled out—two policemen, a social worker, a small Chinese woman, and a sullen-looking boy with an Asian cast to his eyes. He was Carlos, just thirteen years old.

For months, his mother had been trying to travel to Jalteva from San Lorenzo, the southern port city of Honduras, to leave Carlos at the center. Somehow the boy had always managed to escape from her on the trip. This time, to prevent Carlos from escaping once more, she asked the help of a social worker and the two policemen. She seldom had help from her husband, who was a sailor. This was part of Carlos' problem. His father was frequently away on a cargo ship, sometimes for as long as six months at a stretch. Actually, the father had met his wife in a port city along the shipping line. He had managed to bring the woman to Honduras on a return trip.

Carlos didn't want to be at the center. He was accused of having killed a man but claimed his innocence. However, in Honduras, you are guilty until proven innocent. So far, no proof had been found that Carlos had committed the crime. Only circumstantial evidence pointed that way. The boy continued to argue that he had not been near the scene of the crime. He said he didn't even know the man he was supposed to have killed. Despite this, the juvenile court ordered Carlos to Jalteva until he was eighteen.

Knowing that his mother would only bring him back to Jalteva if he ran away, Carlos didn't even attempt this. He also remembered the long, cross-country distance San Lorenzo was from Jalteva. He wasn't sure he could find his way if he did run away, so Carlos decided to settle in at the center and make the most of it. His companions immediately nicknamed him "Chino" because of his Chinese looks.

Carlos chose shoemaking as the trade he wished to learn. He loved the feel of leather and the handling of knives. To begin his formal education, he entered first grade, since he had never gone to school. He wasn't sure he was going to enjoy sitting still in a desk for a half day, following a fixed schedule. This type of discipline was new in his life.

Feeling especially lazy one morning, Carlos decided not to go to classes. The result was a sanction by his professor. Angry at this, Carlos swiftly swiped his hand past the professor's jaw, slashing a deep cut along the jawline. With blood running onto his shirt, the professor tried to staunch the bleeding with one hand while grabbing Carlos' wrist with the other. The professor got to the infirmary, dragging Carlos with him. He plunked the boy down on a chair in the dispensary so he could keep an eye on him while the nurse stitched up the slash. Carlos silently sulked. After a tetanus shot, the professor checked out Carlos. Hidden between two fingers, Carlos had a flattened bottle cap, razor sharp on its edges. That had been his weapon.

From the infirmary Carlos was taken to the director's office. Because he had attacked a professor and injured him, the sanction this time was the most severe handed out in the early years of the center. Carlos was locked in solitary in the dorm closet. This was a regular-sized, airy room, opened to screened windows protected by a decorative, metal grill. Besides storage space, the only furnishing was a mattress on the floor. Stripped down to a pair of shorts, Carlos had to spend fifteen days here in isolation. His hair was cropped down to the scalp. At regular intervals, he was taken out for using the bathroom facilities. His meals were brought to him. Twice a day, the gym teacher took Carlos out for some vigorous exercises or to supervise him doing some cleanup activity while the other boys were in class or shop.

Released from isolation, Carlos returned to his classes and the shoemaking shop. He began carrying a leather-cutting knife in a small sheath he had made. Another boy tattled on him, and the shop master frisked Carlos. No knife was found, only the sheath. The incident was reported at the office. Later, Sister Rose called Carlos and went through his pockets, the waistband of his trousers, and his shoes. Pockets were empty, but the waistband yielded a knife tucked away in the folds. In a hidden slit in one shoe, another smaller knife was found. Both were confiscated.

On another occasion, Carlos exploded into fury when Timoteo, a classmate, flung insulting words at him. Carlos pulled a knife. To defend himself, Timoteo stripped off his belt and with the buckle end, struck a solid wallop across Carlos' head. Carlos slashed out with his knife, marking a light gash across Timoteo's forearm.

Arriving on the scene, Sister Rose separated the two and relieved Timoteo of his belt. Holding out her hand, she waited for Carlos to reluctantly place his knife in it. She seated the two boys, one on each side of the table. Yelling at each other, the two spit out their anger, ending in tears when each admitted his part in the fight. Once peace was made, Sister sent Timoteo to the infirmary but kept Carlos a while longer because of his constant knife carrying. She asked him why he did this, knowing he would always be sanctioned each time he was found with a knife. He answered that he felt naked without a knife in his pocket. He didn't feel like a man if he didn't have the security of a knife at hand.

Carlos' knife-fighting didn't end at this point. This time, though, Jaime beat him to the draw in the shoemaking shop. Instead of getting his own supplies from the storeroom, Carlos had taken Jaime's supply of tacks from his space at the workbench. Angry over this, Jaime took a "Turkish revenge," stabbing Carlos in the buttock with his leather-trimming knife. Again, there was no nurse at the center when Carlos was carried facedown to the infirmary. Sister Rose was called. She pulled the deep wound together and taped a thick gauze compress over it to stop the bleeding. She then called for the driver and the pickup truck, got an infirmary mattress placed in the cargo bed of the truck, and had the boys lay Carlos facedown on the mattress. He was rushed off to Talanga, where the doctor stitched up the stab wound and gave him a tetanus shot. Carlos returned to the center. He spent the next three days face down in complete bed rest. Everyone was hoping he had finally learned the dangers of knives.

In circulation once more and free of knives at least for a while, Carlos traded a brand-new padlock to a friend for two oranges and four bananas. At the lunch formation, Sister Rose called his attention to his doing this. She reclaimed both the padlock and the fruit because such trading was not permitted. Besides, she had just gotten the padlock for Carlos for L. 6.00 ($3.00) a few days before. In a huff, Carlos stormed away from the formation and disappeared. He went into hiding and didn't reappear until suppertime, but he did have the traded fruit to hand over.

When the chicken pox epidemic hit the center, Carlos was one of the first victims. He was covered with the pox blisters and suffered high fevers. He was a miserably sick boy. Once the healing began, he was coated with calamine lotion to calm the irritating itching.

In the cafeteria line, Carlos always had to be watched to keep him moving. He held up the serving line while he searched through the stack of dinner plates until he found his favorite with a rose pattern in the center. He seemed to enjoy his meals so much more when the beautiful rose appeared as he cleared his plate.

One Sunday when Carlos' mother came to visit him, she carried her left arm encased in a cast and supported in a sling. Her explanation of what had happened was a sad story. When she had tried to prevent policemen from taking her second son off to jail, one of them had shot her twice, shattering the bones in her arm. She was unable to complain to authorities, or she would be detained for interfering with an arrest.

The cotton plantation down the road from the center was in a bind. They needed many pickers to save their crop before the rains came. The overseer came to the center to ask for help. He offered to pay the boys who were interested. About fifty signed up, Carlos among them. Very early the next morning, the trucks were there to pick up the boys. Carlos happily climbed aboard, dreaming of what he could buy with money he earned. The trucks carried them off to the fields. No classes. No shop. Days away from the center. A new adventure for Carlos and the others.

By the end of the day, the dream was shattered. Carlos returned with his hands punctured, pierced, and scratched from the prickly cup which held each boll of cotton. His back ached. His neck and arms were burned red from the heat of the sun. And worst of all, he had earned only thirty *centavos ($0.15)* for the day's work. The man was only paying three *centavos ($0.015)* for a pound of cotton. What a rip-off! No wonder they couldn't find pickers. Carlos refused to go back the next day, saying he wasn't a slave. Some of the other boys backed out, too.

At one evening formation with the director, all the boys began to sneak glances off to the sidelines. A small disturbance was going on to the left. Arriving late for the formation, Carlos was trying to slide into line without being seen. The disturbance was caused by what he had brought with him—a big fat possum on a cord. Sister Rose quietly motioned Carlos over. She placed him right in front where everyone could see. After that, she didn't know how much the boys were hearing of what the director was saying. At least the possum looked as if it were taking everything in, as it stood there flicking its ears back and forth.

At Christmastime, the boys filled the library to create Christmas tree ornaments and other decorations. Styrofoam pieces were cut into decorative shapes, painted, and sprinkled with glitter. Cardboard toilet paper rolls were sliced into ring sections, and then painted and covered with glitter. Colored crepe-paper tassels were twisted into fluffy starbursts. Even the clumsier boys did a good job, despite paint on the tables, the floor, and even the tips of noses. Carlos helped, making his unique creative designs. He had paint and glitter all over himself. He could have been hung on the tree to sparkle away in the tree lights, just like one more ornament.

On another day, Carlos tried out other artistic skills. He began to draw and letter on the white support posts in the dormitory. Most were silly, vulgar drawings or sayings. On one figure, he placed the name of a boy with his Spanish nickname, which in English meant "eyes of a hung goat." In a way, it was laughable, because the boy did have bulging eyes. Carlos was given the task of washing all his artwork off the posts. Then he was given a stack of scrap paper, a pencil, and crayons, so he could pursue any further artistic urges.

It was Carlos' turn to clean the cafeteria after each meal for a week with Manuel de Jesus. Carlos placed the water bucket he had filled down at his end by the windows, giving easy access for rinsing off his mop. Manuel de Jesus moved the bucket to his end down by the stage, for his convenience. It became a tug-of-war over the bucket, as it was moved from stage to window, window to stage, and back again.

Carlos lost control first and hit Manuel de Jesus. Mops were dropped and fists replaced them. A professor separated the two boys. Still fuming and grumbling, the two picked up their mops. Carlos returned to the windows and hit the glass louvers with a fast punch, breaking four of them in one shot. He grabbed one pointed piece of glass and stormed back toward Manuel de Jesus.

Sister Rose nabbed Carlos as he tried to rush past her. Sister relieved him of the weapon. She sat him down at a table. Then she called Manuel de Jesus over and sat him down across from Carlos. Both started yelling at each other, calling names, insulting the other's mother, spewing out every vulgar word each could think of. Finally, Sister quieted them down and glares replaced words while Sister spoke. When she asked them to talk out the problem, each began to shout again. Stopping them in midstream, Sister had each one explain the incident. Each one blamed the other. Each wanted the bucket on his end of the hall. When asked if it wouldn't better serve both of their purposes if they placed the bucket in the center of the hall, convenient for both of them, the two sat in stunned silence. They had never thought of that. They actually realized what a silly thing they had been fighting over. Making their peace, they picked up their mops, and Manuel de Jesus placed the offending bucket in the center of the hall. The cleaning of the cafeteria proceeded without further fuss.

Helping with the cultivating of the young sprouting plants in the cornfield, Carlos was busy hoeing away. His companion in the next row kept throwing his weeds into Carlos' row. Reacting angrily, Carlos hit Felipe several times on the leg with the blade of his hoe. The injured leg wouldn't hold Felipe upright, so he had to be carried to the infirmary. After Felipe was patched up, Carlos was called. He had the task of carrying Felipe piggyback style to all his activities—dorm, meals, classes—until Felipe could walk again on his own two feet. The two boys actually became friends during the ordeal.

Independence Day, September 15, was coming up fast. The great Central American hero, Francisco Morazán, was honored on this day. He had been born in Honduras. He had fought hard to form a United States of Central America, but it never came about. During the effort, Morazán was elected president with his capital in El Salvador. Betrayed, Morazán was executed before a firing squad in Costa Rica. Jalteva's choral speaking group was preparing a Morazán poem for the civic presentation. Carlos won the coveted speaking role of Francisco Morazán. Some of his companions didn't think he could do it. But on that day, Carlos performed very well as he proudly spoke Morazán's words.

During his five years at Jalteva, personnel worked continuously with Carlos, trying to help him control his quick rise to anger even over the smallest things. Sometimes he succeeded. He was beginning to hold his anger in check. It helped that his eighteenth birthday was looming on the horizon, and he would soon be leaving the center. He would be graduating from the primary school in November at the end of the school year. It was time for Carlos to return home.

Evaluations were made. Reports were sent to the court. Carlos' mother found a job for him in a shoemaking shop along the docks in San Lorenzo. She registered her son in night school, so he could continue his secondary education. Carlos' biggest problem was going to be keeping his anger in control.

Frequent news of Carlos reached Jalteva from San Lorenzo. He was regularly detained for getting into knife fights, injuring someone, or disturbing the peace—any number of reasons. Yet his mother always bailed him out, paying his fines.

On Carlos' last detention, the police, tired of seeing him brought in, told Carlos to go. So in the dark of night, he turned and ran off. The policemen watched him run. Then one of them raised his rifle and shot Carlos in the back, "la ley de fuga," the right to shoot a fleeing prisoner being the excuse. Carlos would no longer be bothering them or anyone else.

Carlos' mother was heartbroken. She returned to Jalteva, asking if we had any photos of her son that she could have. Sister Rose gave her four photos. One was of Carlos on his last Independence Day at the center as he proudly played his role of Francisco Morazán.

Chapter Eleven

Chepe

A group of new arrivals climbed out of the Junta's Jeep at the main gate of the center. Among the boys was a small, pixie-faced fellow. Big ears stood out on each side of his head. An old, filthy hat was plunked on his tousled head. He was a tiny boy with a long name—Jose Maria Luis Ludovico Benito Andres, named after his grandfathers and his father. But everyone called him "Chepe," a short nickname for Jose.

Chepe was rather uncoordinated, slow in movement, and afraid of everyone, including himself. He had been sent to Jalteva for "protection."

It didn't take long to discover that Chepe was hard of hearing, nearly deaf in his left ear due to an infection and constant ear-boxing on the part of his mother. She also punished him by twisting the tops of his ears, pinching these between thumb and forefinger as she twisted. Both of Chepe's ears were disfigured at the top because of this. The torn muscle had healed up in a bunched-up knot. This was most conspicuous when his hair was cut in the treatment for head lice. Then his ears were very outstanding.

Chepe wouldn't give up his old hat because it was his favorite possession. The hat was boiled, dried in the sun, and returned to Chepe.

On the streets, Chepe had been sexually abused by three men who preyed on him. Escaping one, he was caught by another. He was badly damaged. With the slightest rough activity, Chepe began to hemorrhage and had to be rushed off to the hospital. Distance made this difficult, but it became part of his care. In time, with rest, no aggressive play or activities, and a special diet, this was controlled and Chepe healed.

According to Chepe's papers, he should have been in fourth grade. Testing proved otherwise. He was a slow learner and academically way behind. He was placed in the special education group in first grade. He reacted so slowly to everything that soon the boys dubbed him with a new nickname, "Flash." When called this, Chepe responded—slowly.

Chepe loved books but could not read. He solved this problem by borrowing picture books from the library, looking at the pictures, and inventing his own stories. If he selected more difficult books that caught his interest, he nabbed another boy to huddle with him in a corner to read to him.

In writing and math, Chepe needed a lot of help. Volunteers tutored him. His dorm pals always helped him, patiently sitting with him, tracing letters or checking his sums.

Chepe's memory was also weak and undeveloped. At first, he worked with picture memory cards, charts with ten items on a page. He studied these for a while and then without looking, recited the ten pictures he could recall. Once he conquered the picture charts and began to recognize words, Chepe moved on to word memory charts, repeating the same exercises but with words.

Chepe's motor control was another problem. The psychologist had painted a series of educational games on the cement plaza to help boys like Chepe. Every day, Chepe worked at these exercises. He hopped from circle to circle under the psychologist's supervision, trying to land one-footed in the circles. He was very clumsy at first, losing his balance. Gradually he improved. In a line game, his balance became steady. Playing with a large plastic ball, Chepe dodged it each time it was thrown at him instead of catching it. Overcoming his fear, he finally began to catch it and throw the ball back. He also practiced marching to the rhythms of martial music. It took a lot of time to learn to keep his left foot from tangling with his right foot while stepping to the beat.

It was difficult assigning Chepe to a shop to learn a trade because of his lack of coordination. The gardening instructor took Chepe under his wing. He never gave Chepe a machete for work. He was limited to the use of the hoe and rake and manning the wheelbarrow and the watering can.

Much cabbage was produced in the garden plots. It was served in soups, cooked with ground beef, or boiled in a vinegar sauce. For an additional variety, Sister Rose decided to try a new way to serve cabbage. She made sauerkraut. While fermenting, it reeked all over the kitchen. When it was ready, Sister had the cooks serve it with chunks of wieners in the mix, because pork chops or spare ribs were too expensive. The experiment was offered to the boys, who were left free to try it if they wanted to. When it was Chepe's turn to be served, he said he didn't want any of that "stinky cabbage." Then he spied the chunks of wieners, so he changed his mind. He actually liked the sauerkraut and returned for a second helping.

During the heat of the dry season, cicadas open up with their loud, zinging choruses. The boys had a great time catching them and carrying them around in their pockets. Here the cicadas kept up their song as they tried to escape the dark. Two big, fat cicadas got away from Chepe's pocket while he was in the library. This caused a disturbance because everyone had to dodge the frantically flying and buzzing creatures searching for a way out. One settled on the lock of the door, a favorite resting spot for cicadas. When someone tried to put a key into the lock, the cicada would buzz off right under the nose of the key holder. On this day, Chepe nabbed the cicada on the lock and it was returned to his pocket. The second cicada whizzed past him and out the door, free to enjoy the sunlight and summer heat.

Later, Chepe came to the library all excited. He said a fat, ugly toad was sitting under a lamppost and singing just like a cicada. He wanted Sister Rose to come and see this marvel. Yes, there the toad sat all puffed up. Apparently, it had swallowed a cicada in its search for an insect. The cicada's song gradually weakened when it could no longer rub its wings together. Until that happened, that was one frustrated toad.

Sometimes to celebrate a special holiday, a treasure hunt was organized. Even though he wasn't very clever in finding clues, Chepe loved these events. He slowly followed the other boys in their race to find the next clue.

On one occasion, it was quite comical when Chepe became distracted by a snake slithering through the tall grass. He followed the tail of the snake until it came out of the grass at the base of a tree. Chepe was so disappointed. Here it was, just a large, ordinary garden snake, not an exotic, poisonous snake he had hoped for. Then what a surprise! Looking down, Chepe noticed a colorfully-wrapped bundle tucked away among the roots of the tree. The treasure! Chepe gleefully jumped up and down, shouting. He waved the prize on high like a victory banner just as the other boys breathlessly arrived, following the last clue. Some began to accuse Chepe of cheating, saying he had seen where the treasure had been hidden. But Chepe explained that he had been following a snake and it had led him to this tree. The boys believed him. They crowded around as Chepe opened the treasure, a huge chocolate Hershey bar and a packet of fine-pointed, colored markers.

Sometimes Chepe broke out in a talkative streak. Once he started chattering away, it was hard to stop him. However, understanding his carelesly slurred speech was difficult. He swallowed syllables, lisped through others, and stuttered haltingly at times. Most of the time in his long monologue what he said was pure nonsense.

Mischief and pranks played a part in Chepe's life, too. He relished hiding his companions' things. The temptation was greatest when they were all engrossed in an exciting soccer game, which most played barefooted. The players dropped their shoes along the sidelines so they wouldn't wear them out in rough play. When no one was watching, Chepe gathered the shoes, a pair at a time, and tossed them into the tall grass or the field next to the playing area.

After the game, loud complaints sounded on all sides because the players couldn't find their shoes. With complete innocence spread across his face, Chepe simply watched the commotion, enjoying the confusion. Looking around, one boy noticed Chepe's apparent indifference to the situation and pounced on him, grabbing him by the arm and demanding his shoes. Others soon joined in and they shook Chepe until he almost rattled. At last, giving up, Chepe pointed to the field where he had dumped the shoes. Here Sister Rose entered the scene. She scolded Chepe and sent him to collect the shoes. He had to set each pair by Sister so the boys could each claim his shoes.

One day, Chepe found a baby fox cowering in the corner of the dorm bathroom. He wanted to keep it like a pet puppy. He couldn't be convinced to let the creature go and set it free. It would certainly die if Chepe penned it up. For a while, Chepe hid the baby fox in the bottom section of his clothes cabinet, after punching air holes in the plyboard door. He shared part of his own food or begged scraps from the cooks to feed the animal. Returning from his meal one day, Chepe found the panel open and the fox gone. The lower section was empty and the fox had escaped. Chepe never saw it again.

Another event that Chepe always looked forward to was the annual corn roast. When the new corn was ready, he joined his group in collecting firewood for a bonfire in the corral. Then each boy picked the number of ears of corn he wanted to roast and enjoy. Chepe polished off six ears all by himself. With the wind constantly fanning clouds of smoke over the revelers as they crouched around the fire, their clothing was saturated with the smell of smoke by the time the roast ended.

In the theater club, when a special musical dramatization had auditions, Chepe wanted to be a part of it. He did have a lovely, clear singing voice, but his friends thought he would never be able to remember his lines. The musical was *The Land of Jaujau,* the story of a group of children being tempted to a land of pleasure to freely enjoy all the food and fun they wanted. Once there and snared, life was very different. They were treated as captive slaves. Escape was difficult, almost impossible.

The boys tried out for the parts. Chepe wanted to be Harlequin, the principal character and the soloist. This surprised the others, but they were willing to let Chepe try the role. The actors learned all the songs together and then did trial solos. Chepe practiced and practiced with two of his friends, because he really wanted the part. He could be heard off in a corner singing his melodies and trying to remember the lyrics. When he finally auditioned for the part, he did well and won the role. Nobody outside the drama group knew which actors played the different characters. They held colorful masks in front of their faces during the presentation, singing behind the masks. At the end of the show, the actors came down off the stage, circling the hall and holding their masks to the side so all could see who was who as they sang their last song. The audience gasped when they discovered that Chepe had played the role of Harlequin. The tremendous applause was all this small boy needed to feel completely happy for one very important moment in his life.

Then the unexpected happened. Chepe found a machete and tried to cut the weeds along his garden plot. Sure enough, in one swing, he almost cut off the tip of a finger. It really needed stitching, but again, there was no nurse at the center and no truck to take him to the doctor in Talanga. Sister Rose cleaned up the finger and pulled the cut together, putting butterfly tapes on the cut to hold the tip in place. Then she bandaged it. Chepe kept removing the bandage to show off his wound to anyone interested in looking at it. On the third day, the finger looked so bad that Sister Rose sent him to the doctor.

At the clinic, the doctor gave Chepe an antibiotic medication and a sulphur powder to sprinkle on the injured finger. He gave Chepe a tetanus shot. Chepe reacted to the antibiotic medication and got all swollen up and puffy, so that medication was stopped immediately. Sister just continued with the cleansing and powder sprinkling each day, ordering Chepe to leave the bandage in place. The finger was almost healed when Chepe bumped the finger on the metal frame of his cot, knocking the scab loose and opening the injury again. A new tactic was tried—no more bandages, just cleansing and dusting. Chepe was rigged out with a sling to carry his hand in a protective position so he couldn't use that hand. At last, after a few weeks like that, the finger healed nicely.

Years passed and Chepe was approaching his eighteenth birthday. The problem facing him now was where would he live on leaving the center. In school, he had managed to squeeze by with just below-average grades, completing his primary education. He didn't think he could manage high school. He enjoyed working in the fields, especially in horticulture. He didn't want to return to live with his mother or in his old barrio. The social worker thought maybe the Junta could hire Chepe as a field hand to continue working in the garden project. Scouting around and discussing Chepe's needs, Mario, the agricultural overseer, thought he could spare a small room where Chepe could live if the Junta hired him.

This possible solution was presented to headquarters. The personnel office mulled over the case and thought it could be done. Chepe was hired. He would live in Tablon in the room Mario provided. He would pay a small rental fee to Mario for the room and eat his meals with the personnel at the center.

The plan was approved by the juvenile court. Chepe packed his few belongings and moved to Tablon. Working hard, he earned his wages as a field hand and lived independently. He regularly asked for advice or help in solving problems from the personnel at Jalteva.

After two years, having reached his twentieth birthday, Chepe found a better-paying job at a Mennonite farm in Guaimaca. He said his farewells at Jalteva and moved off on his own. He returned regularly for short visits.

Chapter Twelve

Vardo

The month of April was ending. The entire earth was scorched by the fierce heat of the sun. Dust blew across the sky in high, windy swirls because of the lack of rain. The dry season was at its height and the sun at its hottest.

This was also the season in which Vardo, a sixteen-year-old lad from the coast, was brought to Jalteva. Two soldier-guards had traveled with him from La Ceiba "a la corrida." This was a rugged way of traveling cross-country with a prisoner without sufficient funds—hiking, hitching rides, and begging food and a place to sleep along the way. The three were exhausted, hungry, and thirsty after the five days of such travel.

Vardo was a "Moreno," a Negro group living along the coast which made their living as fishermen or as small shopkeepers along the beaches of the port city of La Ceiba. He was a skinny boy. His body was bruised and beaten from abuses he had suffered during his fifty-five-day stay in a crowded jail cell of La Ceiba's prison. He was practically starved, thin as a shadow, with a lean, hungry look about him.

In prisons in Honduras, the detainees don't get much to eat. If their families do not bring food to the prison each day, prisoners hardly eat. And if food is brought, a good bit of it disappears on its way as it passes from hand to hand from the guards at the entrance gate until it reaches the prisoner.

In the cell where Vardo was lodged, there were no bunks or cots—nothing but a cold dirt floor to curl up on. Sometimes Vardo did find a small space where he might risk lying down. If he did, he might get flattened under a layer of humanity or stepped on. He spent most of his time sitting up against the damp wall. During his days there, he hardly ever had a good sleep. Now, after the long days of travel from La Ceiba to Jalteva, Vardo was dead on his feet.

On arriving, the guards uncuffed Vardo and handed him over. Their mission accomplished, and they were served a good meal before starting their return trip "a la corrida." Vardo stood there, very relieved but silent. He pretended tough indifference, putting on a brave front, but he was afraid and hurting badly inside. When invited, he gladly went to eat the huge meal the cooks set before him.

After eating, Vardo went with Sister Rose to her office. She kept him with her for the rest of the day. She talked to him about the center, the opportunities he would have, and what life was all about in Jalteva. Vardo began to relax, doze a bit, and soon he began talking. He told of his horrible jail time, expressing the fear that he had thought he would die in prison. He had nightmares. He had been accused of a robbery that took place on the docks. He denied that he had participated in the theft. Nothing had been proven. At least he had escaped from that jail where he dreaded each day. He was hopeful in beginning a new life in Jalteva.

Vardo talked about his mother, a seamstress who helped support the family of five other children. His father sold fish in a small marketplace for his uncle, who was a fisherman. The family's main diet was fish.

At Jalteva, Vardo had a hard time eating the daily fare. There seldom were fish to enjoy. Vardo missed these terribly, as well as the other traditional Moreno dishes, a diet so different from that of Jalteva. Vardo was one happy boy when the Ministry of Natural Resources seeded the lagoon with thousands of miniature fish. He could hardly wait until they grew to full size. Then he could again fish and enjoy fish at his meals.

The lagoon became Vardo's special haunt. He was sanctioned many times for going there and fishing without permission. He was a good swimmer, but the rule was the boys could only go to the lagoon with the supervision of a professor. When swimming, it was never alone but always with two or three companions nearby.

Vardo joined the carpenter shop to learn his trade. When he visited the shop the first time, he saw the boys hollowing out two chunks of thick tree trunks to make canoes. Vardo eagerly lent a hand, gouging and burning out the hollow and then filling outside cracks with pitch. He worked patiently at it. When the paddles were fashioned and shaped out of sturdy wood, he could hardly wait for the trial run in the lagoon. He wanted to be part of the first crew.

Swimming was also one of Vardo's favorite pastimes. He felt very much at home in the water. He was fast and skimmed smoothly through the waters in relay and meter races. Many times he was the champion. He won many diving contests, slicing down into the depths of the lagoon with his neat dives.

Returning from the lagoon one day, Vardo brought a long, silver snake, a zumbador, held on a stick. He had found it along the edge of the lagoon. This is a fast, poisonous snake, which makes a buzzing, humming sound when it's disturbed. Well, this one was really humming away, trying to defend itself. Being the dry season, it had come out of its hole seeking moisture in the cool waters of the lagoon.

Tug-of-war was another favorite game of the boys, especially along the riverbanks where the river narrowed before dumping into the lagoon. Here, dressed only in their sports shorts, two teams of sturdy boys formed on either side of the river. Two cattle lassos were knotted together over the river's span. Vardo was responsible for doing the tying. Each team got ready, dug in their heels on the riverbank, and gave a hefty tug. The lassos pulled apart, and both teams got dumped unceremoniously on their backsides. Vardo had to swim out and remedy his error. This time he got it right and the knot held. After three trials, many tugs, a few blisters and rope burns, Vardo's team won all three trials. They pulled the opposing team into the river with a resounding splash each time. The boys on Vardo's team were the champions. They boisterously lined up for their snack-bar prize.

Rope-swinging was loads of fun. Two long lassos were looped and tied securely over the strongest branches of the pine trees that lined the edge of the lagoon at its deepest part. Vardo loved this. With a mighty kickoff and a hearty Tarzan yell, he swung back and forth over the water, released his hold, and plunged into the water, raising a tremendous splash and spraying water on all sides. In competitions, the boy who made the biggest splash was the winner. Vardo seldom won this because he was too skinny.

Gradually getting accustomed to the Jalteva diet, Vardo took an interest in baking. He even thought he might enjoy working in a bakery when he left the center. CARE donated sacks of flour, powdered milk, rice, and oatmeal to the center. Sometimes cans of vegetable oil or puddings were added to the donation. Vardo became Dona Maria's right-hand man in bread-making. His strong muscles were great for kneading the dough. It was a special thrill to punch the air out of the inflated batch of dough after its first and second risings. He loved forming the loaves, buns, and sweet rolls. He watched the oven until all within was a toasty, golden brown, enjoying the delicious aroma that wafted from the baking bread. He was especially proud to be selected often for distributing the delicious breads to the boys at mealtime.

As happened many times at the center, there was a scarcity of materials for taking care of personal hygiene. The boys complained about the lack of soap, toothpaste, and toilet paper. Some compared the present situation to worse ones at other centers where they were before coming to Jalteva. Then, out of the clear blue, Vardo popped up with his contribution.

He said, "Just imagine. When I was in Observation Center, they gave me a piece of harsh, homemade laundry soap as my bath soap. Why, my skin began to turn white as layers were peeled off with every scrubbing!"

Vardo was a natural as a comedian. He joined the theater club and became the principal clown in the group of clowns. He was also excellent at miming. Preparing a mimed drama one day onstage, Vardo remembered the movie seen the night before, *The Blues Brothers*. He strutted up and down across the stage, miming a hard, stoical expression on his face.

Then he spoke between his teeth, repeatedly saying, "I'm a Blues brother."

After reminding Vardo several times to get off the stage so the practice could continue, Sister Rose finally said, "I'll soon turn you into a Blues brother if you don't get off this stage right now."

That caught Vardo's attention and he quickly hopped off the stage.

The next day, Vardo was selected with a group of boys to cut the weeds in the laundry patio. Plying his machete, Vardo uncovered a nest of baby boas—no mother in sight. All the boys dropped their machetes and tried to capture the foot-long babies. As soon as a boy touched one, the tiny snake began to wind itself around his finger. Every attempt at picking them up failed. Vardo ran to the art room to ask for some empty paint jars. The boys had a field day collecting the wiggling creatures, enticing them into the jars. Despite the air holes punched in the lids, all the baby boas died after a few days. They wouldn't eat when the boys tried to feed them. Vardo took his snake to the agricultural collection of insects and field life and added his jar to the exhibit on display there.

Studies, shop, sports, and other activities filled Vardo's days. He was easygoing and happy, entering wholeheartedly into whatever he was doing. Because of good behavior, Vardo earned permission to spend Christmas and New Year at his home with his family. But his parents never had enough money to pay his trip home and then back again to the center, so Vardo could never travel home. He spent these days at the center.

Determined to spend at least one Christmas at home, Vardo saved all his shop earnings for his bus fare. He succeeded and happily left with the other boys for the holidays at home. His joy was almost uncontrollable as he neared the coast again after being away for two years.

Vardo spent his first day strolling along the beach and watching the fishing boats come and go. Then, over the next few days, he helped his father sell fish in the shop. He quietly sat at times with his mother as she sewed, completing new dresses for high society ladies preparing for their New Year's Eve parties. He went out one day with his uncle on the fishing boat. Swimming and enjoying his mother's cooking were the gems of his vacation.

On Christmas Eve, Vardo joined some of his old friends at a party on the docks. He made a handsome picture, dressed in his finest. At the party he danced with many lovely young girls. Then a woman began to offer her charms and flirted outrageously with Vardo. She seemed obsessed, even obnoxious. She annoyed Vardo to no end. He wanted to circulate and enjoy dancing with as many different and pretty girls as possible. He wasn't interested in getting stuck with this pestering woman whose name he didn't even know.

Rejected, the woman planned her malicious revenge. She prepared a special plate of food in a very attractive display. Into the food she sprinkled a drug powder from a ground root used among the Morenos for this purpose. The powder reduced the victim to a vegetative state, completely burning out the brain and making the person crazy without hope of ever recovering.

At a break in the dancing, the woman, all smiles, sidled up to Vardo and coaxed him to accept the plate. Politely and unsuspecting, Vardo sat with other friends who were already eating. He ate some of the food. The woman had disappeared into the crowd but was watching from the sidelines. After enjoying about a quarter of the food, Vardo began to feel odd. He didn't know what was happening. He stopped eating and asked one of his friends to walk home with him. Standing up, Vardo left the rest of the plate, and his friend helped him stagger home to the family beach house.

In the early hours of Christmas Day and to the surprise of his family, Vardo erupted into a violent fury. He went berserk. He raged through the house, knocking things about, shrieking and screaming. Nobody could control him. In stunned horror, his father called the police. It took six of them to subdue Vardo. A blow to the head with a nightstick stunned Vardo, and the police hauled him away. They threw him into a jail cell all by himself. There, Vardo threw himself against the bars, kicked the walls, and caused quite an uproar. The police didn't know what to do with him.

Beside herself, Vardo's mother went to the Junta's center in the city. She spoke to a social worker there, describing the unexplainable situation. The social worker radioed to Tegucigalpa, connecting with the director of the observation center. He telephoned the home of the director of rehabilitation to inform her of the problem. She, in turn, called the police in La Ceiba, asking them to borrow the Junta's Jeep and bring Vardo to the mental hospital at San Felipe. Vardo was sedated, and his father traveled with him and the police. The trip took all day. By nightfall, Vardo was at San Felipe.

Jalteva received the news of the tragedy two days after Christmas. The psychologist went to San Felipe to find out firsthand what was happening. Vardo was in a padded cell and sedated to prevent him from hurting himself and others.

At the time, the doctors only said Vardo's craze was caused by some drug. They didn't know how much he had consumed or what drug it was until the lab tests were returned. They calculated that Vardo had not received a full dose of the drug because sometimes he snapped out of the crazed pattern. If he had taken a full dose, this would not have happened.

By mid-January, Vardo was improving, having longer rational periods. Sister Rose decided to visit him. Armed with oranges, a bag of sweet breads, a liter of milk, some cookies, and a packet of youth magazines and comic books, she met Vardo's nurse, Daniel. Daniel told Sister that today was one of Vardo's good days. He was rational and she could visit with him.

The visit took place in the inner patio of the men's pavilion. Here, the less violent patients were walking back and forth or sitting in a corner mumbling to themselves. They were in all states of dress and undress. Some were taking off all their clothes and parading up and down with their bare butts exposed to the wind. Others hovered nearby, peering at Sister out of curiosity.

When Vardo saw Sister, he ran over and hugged her, so happy to see someone he knew. When he saw the food, he almost moaned in ecstasy. He was so hungry that he simply gobbled the sweet breads, drank the milk, and sucked the juice from three oranges. He was so grateful for the magazines and comic books because he loved to read. At the hospital there was nothing to do to pass the time. Everyone just sat or walked. Sister left the remainder of the food and promised to return soon for another visit.

On the next visit, Sister couldn't see Vardo. He was having a bad day and was in a padded cell. Daniel updated Sister on Vardo's progress. He also accepted the food and magazines she had brought for Vardo. Daniel suggested that she bring smaller amounts more frequently because Vardo had no place to hide his food or magazines. Other patients watched closely and when they saw Vardo with food, they descended on him like vultures and swiped his food or stole his magazines.

To resolve the problem, Sister Rose planned with Sister Maria at Casa Santa Teresita. She left magazines, comic books, and money with Sister Maria, who then bought food, milk, or juices and took them to Vardo every other day at San Felipe. Doing this, Vardo could enjoy the food immediately and quickly read his two or three magazines before other fingers snatched them away.

Vardo was so grateful for not being forgotten. He improved week after week. By April, he seemed to have recovered completely. He was released from San Felipe. Vardo was now eighteen, so his parents came to take him home. Returning to La Ceiba, he joined the army.

On one of her free days in Tegucigalpa, Sister Rose was called to the door at Casa Santa Teresita to receive a visitor. There stood Vardo in full uniform, a tall, handsome soldier. He was all smiles. He was on leave and wanted to personally thank Sister Rose and Sister Maria for all the visits, food, and reading material. These had helped him recover his sanity at San Felipe. He felt so blessed for having survived the malicious revenge attempt against him and for knowing the Sisters.

Conclusion

After having shared the stories of these twelve boys whose lives I have touched in some small way, I feel deeply grateful for having had the privilege of caring for and mothering thousands of boys with similar problems during my thirty-one years of service at Jalteva.

Having watched ruined and broken lives be reborn and then recovering, and growing under tender nurturing, I'm filled with a warmth only small miracles gifted from God can give. I cherish all the memories of these young men and their struggles to rebuild and sustain a solid, responsible life with a secure place in present-day society.

Printed in the United States
107661LV00001B/119-268/P

9 781414 111087